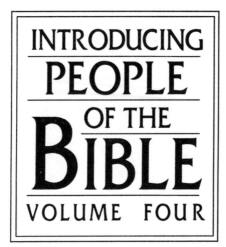

# INTRODUCING
# PEOPLE
## OF THE
# BIBLE
## VOLUME FOUR

# Also by John Phillips

*Exploring Genesis*
*Exploring the Psalms*
*Exploring Proverbs*
*Exploring the Song of Solomon*
*Exploring the Book of Daniel*
(by John Phillips and Jerry Vines)
*Exploring the Minor Prophets*
*Exploring the Gospels: John*
*Exploring Acts*
*Exploring Romans*
*Exploring Ephesians*
*Exploring Philippians*
*Exploring Hebrews*
*Exploring Revelation*

*Exploring the Future*
*Exploring the Scriptures*
*Exploring the World of the Jew*
*Bible Explorer's Guide*

*Introducing People of the Bible, Volume 1*
*Introducing People of the Bible, Volume 2*
*Introducing People of the Bible, Volume 3*

*100 Sermon Outlines from the Old Testament*
*100 Sermon Outlines from the New Testament*
*Sermon Outlines on the Psalms*

*Only One Life: A Biography of Stephen Olford*

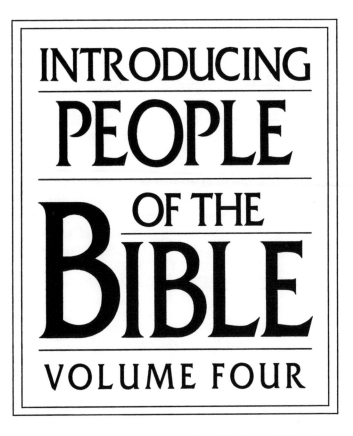

# INTRODUCING
# PEOPLE
## OF THE
# BIBLE
## VOLUME FOUR

# JOHN PHILLIPS

**LOIZEAUX**
Neptune, New Jersey

***INTRODUCING PEOPLE OF THE BIBLE, VOLUME 4***
*© 1999 by John Phillips*

*A Publication of Loizeaux Brothers, Inc.,*

A Nonprofit Organization Devoted to the Lord's Work
and to the Spread of His Truth

*All Scripture quotations, unless otherwise noted, are
from the King James version.*

*Library of Congress Cataloging-in-Publication Data
(Revised for vol. 4)*

*Phillips, John, 1927–
Introducing people of the Bible.
1. Bible—Biography.    I. Title.
BS571.P52  1991    220.9'2    91-39819
ISBN  0-87213-626-4*

*Printed in the United States of America*

*10  9  8  7  6  5  4  3  2  1*

# Contents

# 1
# Noah
# and His Ark

*Hebrews 11:7*

```
I. NOAH'S CONVERSION
II. NOAH'S CALL
III. NOAH'S COURAGE
IV. NOAH'S CONVERTS
V. NOAH'S CONSCIENCE
```

The storm had been brewing for some fifteen hundred years. Signs of that coming storm were evident, not in the skies of heaven, but in the sins of humanity. Callousness, corruptness, and crime were the indicators.

If we were to measure progress in terms of social dynamics, scientific development, and successful discovery, we would have to say that the people of Noah's day had taken enormous strides forward. God, however, does not measure progress in terms of how bold, brilliant, and businesslike men are. He uses a different yardstick altogether. When He looked at antediluvian society, He "saw that the wickedness of man was great" (Genesis 6:5).

As the storm approached, the world became increasingly urban; cities sprang up everywhere. Moreover the equivalent of an industrial revolution transformed the way people lived. They became more sophisticated, permissive, and worldly. A women's liberation movement encouraged many women to put aside home-related responsibilities and enter the mainstream of life. Liberal ideas about human rights undermined traditional values and consequently lawlessness, vice, and violence were widespread.

Side by side with an increasing sophistication in the arts and sciences was an increasing fascination with the weird, the supernatural, and the uncanny. Some people delved so deeply into forbidden secrets that they were actually able to spawn a hybrid progeny that was part human, part supernatural (Genesis 6:1-4; 2 Peter 2:4; Jude 6). As a result of these occult practices, human degeneration accelerated.

Then too there was such a population explosion that the corresponding increase of immorality could only be measured in terms of geometric progression. No wonder a storm was coming. It was a storm of such magnitude and horror that when it was over, God pledged never again to judge the world in that way.

In the midst of all this corruption, Noah sought to live for God. Let us think about this man and the impact he made—or failed to make—on his society, for our society is much the same as his.

# I. NOAH'S CONVERSION

Noah came from a family that had a tradition of godliness. He stood in the direct line of a succession of godly men reaching back to Seth, the son of Adam, to whom God entrusted the Messianic promise. Noah's father, grandfather, and great-grandfather were prophets, and before them, Noah's forebears had been patriarchs. Generation after generation, fathers had faithfully handed the torch of testimony to their sons.

Noah was brought up to cherish the great truths of Scripture as they were known and transmitted in those far-off times. He knew about creation and the fall. He knew that sin and death had entered the world because of one man's disobedience. Having heard about Cain and Abel, Noah understood that "without faith it is impossible to please [God]" (Hebrews 11:6) and that man is not justified on the basis of good works. Noah knew that "the way of Cain" (Jude 11)—the way of dead religion that focuses on human merit—was fathered by Satan, is furthered by violence, and will be finalized in the lake of fire. Noah knew about Enoch, who walked with God so closely that his translation to Heaven was by way of rapture rather than by way of death.

Noah's family taught him Biblical truth, but that did not make him a child of God. Being born into a godly family is not the same as being born into God's family. Noah had to be born again. We know that eventually he experienced the new birth because Genesis 6:8 tells us that he "found grace in the eyes of the Lord."

Before any of us can find that grace, we must first see ourselves as sinners in need of the Savior. A man who imagines himself to be well is not likely to seek a doctor. In a similar way, as long as we imagine that we are good enough for God, we are unlikely either to find or to accept God's grace.

The word translated "grace" in the Bible does not refer to some kind of personal charm, or a pleasing and thoughtful disposition, or an agile bearing. It refers to unmerited favor. God's grace reaches out to lost and ruined people and offers them His love, kindness, and forgiveness instead of His wrath and judgment. We receive something we do not deserve.

Noah saw himself as a sinner, but found that his sins could be forgiven, that he could be received into the family of God, and that he could have the very life of God bestowed on him. In other words, he discovered God's way of salvation. The fact that he "found" grace reveals that he was a seeker. When a seeking sinner meets a seeking Savior, the result is a life-transforming conversion. So Noah was saved, born again, regenerated.

Let us backtrack to a time before he was converted and picture six-year-old Noah climbing up on Methuselah's knee and saying, "Grandpa, how old are you?"

"Oh, I'm not very old. I'm what you would call middle-aged. I'm 375 years old. I'm just 10 years older than my father Enoch was when God took him home to Heaven."

"You mean he died, Grandpa?"

"No, Noah, my father did not die. He was a godly man and walked with God for 300 years. He was saved when he was 65, the very year I was born, and walked with God from then on."

"You mean he was religious, Grandpa? He went to 'church' and things like that?"

"No, it was much more than that, Noah. He knew God personally. Enoch talked to Him as friend to friend. And he allowed nothing in his life that would displease God."

"Why did he name you *Methuselah*, Grandpa?"

"When I was born, God told Enoch that when I die, He intends to send judgment on the earth. The name *Methuselah* means 'When he dies, it shall come.'"

We can almost see Noah's eyes grow wide and we can imagine that after that conversation he would watch his grandfather closely—"Are you feeling good today, Grandpa? You don't have any aches or pains, do you? Is your heart beating good and strong?" A realization that the holy God had already set the date when He would judge the sinful world crept over young Noah's soul. The more he thought about that prospect, the more he realized that he was sinful. But the day came when he sought and found grace in the eyes of the Lord.

## II. NOAH'S CALL

The acid test of whether or not we are truly saved is whether or not our lives have changed. It is true that we cannot do anything to be saved except trust in the Lord Jesus Christ, but it is equally true that we cannot be saved and do nothing.

When Saul of Tarsus met the risen Christ on the Damascus

road, he immediately asked, "Who art thou, Lord?" (Acts 9:5) With that one word, "Lord," he threw down the arms of rebellion and opened his soul to Jesus, the Son of God. Saul's next statement put meaning, reality, and purpose into the surrender of his soul to the Savior. "Lord," he said, "what wilt thou have me to do?" (9:6) Right from the start he realized that by becoming a Christian he was putting his whole life at the disposal of Christ.

Likewise when Noah was saved, God called him to his lifework. There was a job for him to do—an enormous, costly, all-consuming task that had global and eternal significance. God has a lifework for each of us as well. As the old chorus puts it:

> There's a work for Jesus ready at your hand,
>  'Tis the task the Master, just for you has planned;
> Haste to do His bidding, yield Him service true,
>  There's a work for Jesus none but you can do.
> > (Elsie Duncan Yale)

God called Noah to build an ark "to the saving of his house" (Hebrews 11:7). Noah's salvation hinged on his finding grace in the eyes of the Lord; the salvation of Noah's children hinged on his obedience to God's call.

If Noah was anything like us, he was probably aghast when he received God's call. We can almost hear him protest:

> Me, Lord? Build an ark? Why me? Why not one of the Cainites? They have a monopoly on the mechanical arts. They know all about smelting, engineering, and building. We Sethites are separated from the Cainite way of life. If I were to start building an ark, I'd have to hire designers, craftsmen, shipwrights, smiths, and carpenters. I'd have to build forges and warehouses. I don't know anything about construction.
>
> Besides, where would I get the money? I have no

idea what this ark is going to cost, but it is hard enough
to make ends meet as it is. Lord, You know I don't have
any money. There are no industrialists or bankers in our
family.

And You say that You want me to put all kinds of
animals in this ark when it is finished. How would I
catch two lions, two tigers, two boa constrictors, two of
every kind of bird, and two of every kind of insect? I
don't know anything about rounding up wild animals.
Besides, how would I ever keep them fed and watered
for months on end while the storms of judgment roll?

I'm sorry, Lord. I'll do anything you want me to do—
except build an ark.

God, however, kept reminding Noah that the ark would
be "to the saving of his house." An important principle is
illustrated here. How can we expect our children to be obedient
if we aren't obedient? When Christian parents grieve over a lost
child who has rebelled against God, His Word, His Son, and His
church, they wonder where he learned to rebel. Quite often a
child learns at home from parents who have been rebellious in
some area of life.

The Lord's only answer to the excuses Noah probably
made was, "Make thee an ark" (Genesis 6:14). At last Noah
ceased protesting and, driven by God's unchanging demand,
accepted the call and began his task. He had to hew out giant
timbers, saw them down to size, and construct the ark's massive
frame. He had to measure off the rooms, cages, and storage
areas. And he had to boil huge vats of pitch. So it was that Noah
began an enormous work for God, a work that was a gigantic
testimony to the people of his day.

## III. NOAH'S COURAGE

It took courage to build that ark. We can imagine what
kind of coverage the project would have received if there had

been a local newspaper. Interviews with enterprising reporters would have sounded something like this:

"Hello, Noah. I'm writing an article about you for the newspaper and I thought I'd stop by for an interview. I understand you're building some kind of boat."

"That's right."

"Judging by all these timbers you have stacked up in the yard and what you've already done, I gather that the boat is going to be big."

"Yes."

"How big?"

"About the size of a city block."

"That's some boat! What shape is it going to be?"

"The shape of a coffin."

"A coffin? You've got to be kidding."

"No. It's going to be three hundred cubits long, fifty cubits wide, and thirty cubits high. That's just about the same shape as a coffin."

"You mean you're building a coffin the size of a city block?"

"Yes—only it's an ark, not a coffin."

"What is an ark?"

"A coffin is for dead people; an ark is for living people. Everyone in my ark will live and everyone outside my ark will die."

"Oh come on, Noah! I've always known that there is a strong streak of religious mania in your family, but I never thought religion could make a person go to such fantastic extremes as this."

"I am both sane and serious."

"Why are you building the ark here, Noah? I don't see any mechanism for getting it into the water. How are you going to launch it? Are you going to carry it on camels or something?"

"No, that won't be necessary."

"It won't be necessary?"

"No. You see, I will not have to carry this ark to the water. The water will come to the ark."

"Oh come off it, Noah! You can't be serious."

"I'm absolutely serious."

"All right, so the ocean is going to come to the ark and pigs might fly. What else is going to happen?"

"It's going to rain. In fact there is going to be a deluge unlike any other in the history of the world."

"Well, thanks for the tip, Noah. I think I'll buy some shares in an umbrella factory. Now, how many people do you think will take a ride in this big boat of yours?"

"I don't know."

"You mean you're building a ship of this size and you're just hoping that people will ride in it? Has anyone signed up yet?"

"Only my family."

"How much are you going to charge?"

"Nothing."

"Now I know you're kidding. Just these materials that I can see here must have cost plenty. You must be going to charge something for a seat in this floating barn of yours when you open up for business."

"I'm quite serious. There will be no charge for a place in the ark. Everything will be provided free. Would you like me to make a reservation for you?"

"I'll think about it. By the way, where's all the money coming from? As far as I know, there are no wealthy men in your family. Have you been robbing a bank or something?"

"God has supplied all my needs."

"I don't believe that."

"Please yourself, but it's true just the same."

"Well, when is this deluge you speak of supposed to start?"

"I don't know, but it won't be until the ark is finished."

"I see you're building many cages and cubicles. What are they for?"

"The animals."

"What animals?"

"The animals that will be saved from the flood by taking refuge in the ark."

"Man, this gets crazier and crazier. How many animals?"

"I don't know. There will be two of each kind of wild animal and seven of each kind of clean animal."

"Clean animals! How do you decide which ones get the bath?"

"Clean animals are those that have divided hoofs and chew the cud."

"So you're going to cage up in this boat a menagerie of cows, camels, pigs, porcupines, birds, and bees? I've never heard of anything so crazy in my life. Well, thanks for the interview, Noah. I was going to publish my article as a news item, but I think I'll put it with the comic strips."

If there had been a newspaper, Noah's ark would have made the front page. We can picture the headlines: "Lunatic Builds Boat. Says It's Going to Rain." Surely the ark was the talk of the town. People no doubt scoffed at Noah and called him names, but he kept on building his ark. Others probably ignored him. Perhaps there were some who tried to vandalize the work and maybe the zoning officials threatened to lock him up. However, with magnificent courage Noah persevered.

## IV. NOAH'S CONVERTS

Noah, we are told, was "a preacher of righteousness" (2 Peter 2:5). While he was building the ark—and that was a very long time—he warned the world of judgment to come and proclaimed that God's grace had provided salvation for everyone. Noah preached for about 120 years—by the roadside and from door to door, in giant crusades and in the open air. He used all the media of his day to tell people that God was outraged by their sin and that judgment was on the way.

But his only converts were his wife, his sons, and their

wives. Not a single person outside his family paid the slightest attention to what he had to say.

Then Methuselah died. Certainly many people attended his funeral because he was somewhat of a celebrity, being the oldest man in the world. Surely Noah preached at that funeral, and it might well have been his last sermon.

"Come!" we can hear him say. "The storm clouds are gathering. The signs of the times are upon us. Methuselah has died and you all know what his name means: 'When he dies, it shall come!' Now he is dead and it is coming. The ark awaits you and there's nothing to pay. All things are ready. Come just as you are!"

But one and all, the mourners went away—some sobered, some scoffing, some deeply stirred. Not one came forward to accept a place in the ark.

## V. NOAH'S CONSCIENCE

Noah and his family, however, believed God. They took the step of faith and entered the ark. The next seven days nothing happened and Noah's critics must have hooted and howled. Little did they know that they were sinning away the last precious moments of the day of grace.

Then the storm came and the people came, beating on the ark. We can almost hear their cries: "Noah, I'm your foreman." "Noah, I carried the pitch." "Noah, open the door!"

But it was too late. Noah had embarked for another world. He had clean hands, a pure heart, and "a conscience void of offense." Their blood was on their own heads. He was "pure from the blood of all men." (See Psalm 24:4; Acts 24:16; 18:6; 20:26.)

# 2
# Ham
# and His Sin

*Genesis 5:32; 7:13; 10:6*

---

I. WHEN HAM LIVED
   A. An Age of Discovery
   B. An Age of Darkness
   C. An Age of Demonism
   D. An Age of Danger

II. WHOM HAM LIKED

III. WHAT HAM LEARNED

IV. WHAT HAM LOST

V. WHAT HAM LEFT
   A. A Vigorous Family
   B. A Victorious Family
   C. A Villainous Family

---

The Bible tells us that Ham was one of Noah's sons, that he was married, and that he founded a vigorous and brilliant family. We also know from Scripture that because Ham did something shameful to his father, God passed him over for blessing in favor of his brothers, and one of his sons felt the full weight of God's curse.

Ham had an older brother and a younger brother.[1] That may be significant. Sometimes a middle child feels unimportant and neglected. The oldest child in a family often receives a lot of attention and praise. In fact in many cultures the oldest son is the heir and he is given pre-eminence and power. Usually the youngest child in a family also receives plenty of attention—and less stern discipline. Mothers and fathers tend to spoil the baby of the family. Thus the middle child may feel that he doesn't receive his due deserts. He could use a little more of the praise that the older sibling monopolizes and a little more of the pampering the younger one enjoys.

Perhaps that was Ham's problem. Certainly he caused his father more headaches and more heartache than the other two boys combined. And he didn't amount to anything spiritually.

That is about all the Bible says about Ham, but it is enough. We may not be able to picture all the details, all the flesh tones, and all the features of this Bible character, but we have enough information to form an acceptable silhouette in our minds. Let us begin our study of Ham by considering the age in which he lived.

# I. WHEN HAM LIVED

## A. An Age of Discovery

Ham lived during an exciting and exotic time in world history. It was an age of scientific discoveries and high technology. Astonishing new inventions affected life on the farm and life in the city. There seemed to be no end of developments in metallurgy, music, and marketing. The introduction of previously undreamed-of weapons changed the whole concept of war. Cities sprang up and urban life boomed.

Great things were happening, but they had unfortunate results that broke the heart of God.

## B. An Age of Darkness

Progress in the arts and sciences and the development of new skills in engineering and technology do not do much to feed the soul. In fact emphasis on material things blunts the edge of spiritual awareness. It is not surprising therefore to discover that Ham lived in an age of general disbelief.

People prided themselves on living in an age of reason, but the great truths that had been committed to men by divine revelation and handed down by faithful men from generation to generation were either forgotten or laughed out of court. The teachings about the fall of man, the nature of sin, the need for righteousness, the salvation offered by God, the substitutionary/sacrificial atonement, and the nearness of judgment had long ago been tossed aside.

After the rapture of Enoch, God had to search the planet to find just one outstanding man who really believed and could therefore be called righteous. Noah appears to have been the one man who stood for God and dared to preach boldly to a lost world during those dark days. Although Ham probably did not think so, he was fortunate to have such a godly father.

## C. An Age of Demonism

By ignoring vital spiritual truths, the builders of antediluvian society created a vacuum. One of the first principles of physics I learned as a boy was that nature abhors a vacuum. If a vacuum is created in the physical world, something will rush in and fill it. Likewise if the truth of God is taken away from men, the lies of Satan will immediately fill the void. People have to believe something. If they don't believe God's Word, they will believe man's word or a myth that Satan has concocted.

Our society too ignores spiritual truth. Like the people of Ham's day, we live in an age of science and superstition. Never before has man known so much about the nature of the physical universe. We have the technology to explore the moon and incinerate our planet. Yet hundreds of radio and television talk shows feature psychics, witches, and occultists. Their prognostications are false, but as long as these individuals are sensational they can command large audiences of gullible people.

Modern man is both an intellectual giant and a moral pygmy. People were the same in Noah's day. They were wrapped up in the occult, demonism, and spiritism and could produce astonishing phenomena that could deceive the very elect. Such diabolical practices were later put under the curse of God (Leviticus 20:6,27).

What the Bible calls the deep things of Satan are outlawed by God's Word. Those who practice spiritism and demonism, who advance beyond the frauds and initial stages, do indeed establish contact with evil spirits. These iniquitous supernatural beings serve Satan and deceive men. Some of them have great power, which they share with their human partners. A society that rejects Scripture invariably accepts false religious teachings that are Satanic in origin, but coated with enough sugar to make them desirable.

### D. An Age of Danger

"Liberty!" was the cry of the age. Lawlessness was the consequence. According to Genesis 4–6 people abandoned the traditional standards of right and wrong, and everybody did "his own thing." A sexist and feminist movement gained strength and old-fashioned laws concerning marriage were thrown aside (4:19,23-24). Pornography was taken for granted and no one expected the city streets to be safe. "The earth was filled with violence" (6:11) and the thoughts of men's hearts were "only evil continually" (6:5).

## II. WHOM HAM LIKED

Two kinds of people lived during the days of Ham: Cain's kind of people and Seth's kind of people. Cain was the forerunner of the worldly, godless, secular crowd. Seth, on the other hand, was the founder of the godly line into which Ham was born. This believing remnant sought fellowship with God and wanted to live for Him. They were an ever-decreasing minority, a Gulf Stream in an icy ocean of men who had no use for God.

Noah's middle child shared the interests of the ungodly, as his subsequent behavior revealed. Alexander Whyte painted this portrait of Ham:

> There was an old vagabond, to vice industrious, among the builders of the ark. He had for long been far too withered for anything to be called work; and he got his weekly wages just for sitting over the pots of pitch and keeping the fires burning beneath them.... It was of him that God had said that it grieved and humbled Him at His heart that He had ever made man. The black asphalt itself was whiteness itself beside that old reprobate's heart and life. Now Ham, Noah's second son, was never away from that deep hollow out of which the preparing pitch boiled and smoked. All day down among the slime-pits, and all night out among the sultry woods—wherever you heard Ham's loud laugh, be sure that lewd old man was either singing a song there or telling a story.[2]

Although the coloring in Whyte's portrait is imaginative, Ham's life and character provide evidence that he gravitated more readily to the haunts of the ungodly than to the place of prayer.

Ham had every spiritual advantage. People like him are born into the homes of godly parents in every age. They are raised where God's Word is revered, His throne is implored, and His will is supreme. From childhood on, they are taught the gospel, yet they are beguiled by this evil world.

Some children who are born into Christian homes resent their parents' strict standards. These youngsters are ruled by the lust of the eye, the lust of the flesh, and the pride of life (1 John 2:16). What the world offers, appeals to them. They think they are being robbed because their parents seek to protect them from the world and its ways. Such children prefer godless friends and sneak off with them because they crave a sly drink and a puff or two at a cigarette or a joint of marijuana, or because they want to see a filthy movie. They are traitors to the truth of God and rebels against the grace of God. They rebel because God placed them in choice families where they could have learned to love the Lord. They wish they had been born into godless homes where irksome restraints are unknown.

Ham was like them. He was much more attracted to the Cainites than he was to the people of God. The Cainites were exciting, uninhibited, and fun to be around. The Sethites had too many restrictions. Bible conferences and prayer meetings seemed dull to Ham and evangelistic meetings were embarrassing. The Cainites read books that pandered to the flesh; the Sethites contented themselves with God's truth. The Cainites experimented with sex and made fun of sin; the Sethites maintained high moral standards and fought against fleshly lusts that war against the soul (1 Peter 2:11). Ham preferred the ungodly Cainite way of life.

## III. WHAT HAM LEARNED

According to the Bible, Ham's father was "a preacher of righteousness" (2 Peter 2:5). Probably Noah preached in his home as much as he did anywhere else. No doubt he declared that righteousness is *required*. The eyes of the holy God are too pure to look on iniquity. Sin is an offense against His laws. God would have to abdicate His throne if He ever ceased to demand righteousness as the standard for all behavior. God can, does, and must punish sin, and the penalty is death.

When Noah preached to his generation, doubtless he warned them that conditions had become so corrupt that God was preparing to step into the arena of human affairs and judge the world in wrath. We can hear him cry, "Flee from the wrath to come!"

Since man is absolutely incapable of producing the required righteousness, Noah certainly preached that God had provided a way for man to *receive* righteousness. Noah would have said, "There is none righteous, no not one. There is none that doeth good, no not one." And to prove he was right, he would have pointed to man's venomous tongue, violent temper, vile tastes, and vicious tendencies.

No doubt Noah used the story of Cain and Abel—still fresh in the minds of men—to teach that salvation is not earned by human effort. He would have said, "We are not saved by works of righteousness that we have done. Our righteousness is like a filthy rag in God's sight. But God will count faith as righteousness. He will accept faith as substitute. All He requires is that we believe."

In Ham's day it was necessary for a person to demonstrate his faith by going into the ark. Only then would he receive salvation. He had to acknowledge his lost condition and deliberately accept the salvation that God provided. Noah preached the same gospel that we preach—only in his day the ark was the symbol, whereas today Christ is the substance.

Noah was far too good a preacher to stop there. He would have gone on to say that the proof of genuine salvation is a changed life and a changed love. The believing man will love what he once loathed and loathe what he once loved. In other words, righteousness must be *reproduced* in him. He must have a belief that behaves. True salvation of the soul results in sanctification of the life.

Ham heard Noah preach hundreds of sermons. As the end of the age drew near and the signs of the times began to multiply, Noah's voice became more urgent. Even Ham had to stop and think. Finally he decided to take the step of faith and so we read, "In the selfsame day entered Noah, and Shem, and Ham, and Japheth, the sons of Noah, and Noah's wife, and the

three wives of his sons with them, into the ark" (Genesis 7:13).
Note the use of the polysyndeton (the deliberate repetition of
the word "and") in that verse. Every time the conjunction is
used, it draws attention to one item in the list. Noah went in
the ark; that was his choice. Shem went in; that was his choice.
Japheth went in; that was his choice. Noah's wife went in; that
was her choice. The other three women went in; that was their
choice. Ham went in; that was his choice.

No one pushed Ham into the ark. God convicts, but He
does not coerce. Salvation is a personal choice and Ham chose
to enter the ark. However, Ham did not go in with an undivided
heart. He took the world, the flesh, and the lusts of his heart
with him. He paid scant attention when Noah made the point
that righteousness must be reproduced. Ham's motivation for
accepting salvation was fear. He did not want to perish. He
had little knowledge of or concern for the responsibilities of
faith.

## IV. WHAT HAM LOST

Some people will be saved, "yet so as by fire" (1 Corinthians 3:15). In other words, they will be saved, but barely. We
meet numerous examples in the Bible. One is Abraham's
nephew Lot. He stepped out in faith with his uncle at the
beginning of Abraham's pilgrimage and seemed to do well for
a while, but before long he fell by the wayside. The good seed
of the Word of God had fallen among the thorns in his soul (see
Matthew 13:7,22). The last time we see Lot in the Old Testament, he is drunk and dishonored on the hills overlooking the
smoking ruins of Sodom. Were it not for the comment in
2 Peter 2:7-8, we would doubt that Lot was ever saved at all.
He was saved, "yet so as by fire."

The same was true of Ham. He was saved—he entered the
ark—but we comb his life in vain for any evidence of
sanctification. Nothing but the vast, incomparable, wonderful
grace of God could have counted him saved.

Ham discredited his father, one of the greatest of all God's saints, when he found Noah drunk and naked (Genesis 9:20-27). We can make excuses for the old gentleman and give him the benefit of the doubt. Perhaps he did not know that under the new climatic conditions after the flood, grape juice would ferment into wine. Be that as it may, when Shem and Japheth heard about their father's sad condition, they walked backward into his presence so as not to look upon his shame and quietly and tactfully covered Noah with a blanket. These two men had drunk deeply of the grace of God and knew something about the compassion of Christ. In them righteousness was reproduced. Ham, however, had no such scruples. He looked. He gloated. He ran out to broadcast the news. There was no love or respect in this crude man. Love covers a multitude of sins, but gossip runs for the telephone.

We do not know what else Ham did. The inference is that he and his son Canaan were guilty of even worse misconduct. All we know for sure is that a short time later, with the flood tide of divine inspiration upon him, old Noah soundly cursed Canaan. The severity of the curse suggests sin far worse than a mocking look and a gossiping tongue. Noah blessed Japheth. He blessed Shem. He looked at Ham and then did what Ham had not done—he looked away. Having no blessing for Ham, Noah passed over him in eloquent silence. He neither blessed Ham nor cursed him.

Thus Ham lost the blessing of God. There would be enlargement for Japheth and enlightenment for Shem, but nothing for Ham. He went through life unblessed and entered eternity unrewarded. He had a saved soul but an impoverished life.

To miss the blessing of God is a terrible loss for a child of God. God has promised rich blessings for His people, but most of those promises require a response on our part (see for instance Exodus 20:12; Ephesians 6:2-3). The greatest blessing He has for us in this life is to increase our capacity for Christ for all eternity.

# V. WHAT HAM LEFT

Everyone leaves something behind when he dies. Some believers leave money to be squandered by unsaved relatives. Other Christians leave new believers who will carry on the faith for another generation. One man may leave a legacy of books he has written and another may leave buildings he has designed. Some people leave a legacy of misery and others leave debts for relatives to pay. Still others leave divided churches or false teachings.

To find out what Ham left behind, we need to look at what Scripture and secular history tell us about three of his sons: Mizraim, Cush, and Canaan. They founded three prominent families.

## A. A Vigorous Family

Mizraim was the father of the Egyptians, the first great empire-builders on this planet. We still stand in awe of the mighty monuments built on the sands of Egypt. For centuries the pyramids have stood there, defying the gnawing tooth of time. They represent the magnificent civilization that flourished along the Nile in the days of the pharaohs.

That civilization with all its pageantry and power was based on gross superstition and was obsessed with thoughts of death. The Egyptians worshiped cats, cows, crocodiles, bats, beetles, birds, and other beasts. So Ham left behind a legacy of worldly magnificence utterly bereft of spiritual sanity and totally devoid of any real knowledge of God.

## B. A Victorious Family

Cush's son Nimrod founded two of the greatest cities of antiquity: Nineveh and Babylon. Nineveh, which became the capital of the Assyrian empire, was the home of every kind of cruelty. Babylon, which became the capital of the Babylonian empire, was the home of every kind of cult. These cities dominated Biblical history for centuries as they campaigned against the interests of God in this world.

The Assyrians, Babylonians, and Egyptians specialized in persecuting the people of God. What a legacy for a saved man—a man who knew what it was like to be in the ark when the world was being scoured by the waters of God's wrathful judgment—to bequeath to posterity!

## C. A Villainous Family

Canaan was the founder of the Canaanite civilization. This son of Ham had somehow absorbed all the filth of the antediluvian world. Since Canaan had never lived in that world, he must have imbibed its spirit from his father. The horrid sins that brought about the flood were all reproduced in Canaan and his sons. They developed a pornographic society that exalted immorality and sexual perversion as the highest acts of religious worship. Their civilization became so vile that God had to decree its extermination in the days of Moses and Joshua.

We wonder how such children could come out of the home of a man like Ham, who once knew a real experience of salvation! It must have broken old Noah's heart to see the kind of people Ham was bringing into the world.

Ham does not seem to have lost an hour's sleep over the behavior of his offspring. He was saved, but not sanctified. He thought he could live for both worlds. He lived as if there had never been a person such as Noah, a vessel such as the ark, or a judgment such as the flood, and as if there would be no accountability at the judgment seat of Christ.

Next to an out-and-out sinner, there is no more dreadful person on this planet than an all-out backslider. In some ways he is more miserable than the person who openly espouses atheism, immorality, and violence. The person who is saved but who does not show the slightest interest in the gifts and callings of God, cannot possibly be happy. His salvation prevents him from enjoying what this world has to offer and his efforts to live for this world prevent him from enjoying "the powers of the world to come" (Hebrews 6:5).

When we look at Ham, we should tremble. Paul trembled, fearing that having preached to others, he might end up on one of God's rubbish heaps—totally useless for the work of God and a stumbling block for others (1 Corinthians 9:27).

---

1. "Younger" in Genesis 9:24 means younger than Japheth, not younger than Shem. See marginal notes for Genesis 5:32 and 10:1 in _The Companion Bible_ (Grand Rapids: Zondervan, 1974). Especially note the comments on textual structure.

2. Alexander Whyte, _Bible Characters: Adam to Achan_ (Edinburgh: Oliphant Anderson and Ferrier, 1898) 80.

# 3
# Nimrod
# and His Tower

*Genesis 10:8-12; 11:1-9*

---

I. THE CONNECTIONS NIMROD CULTIVATED
II. THE CONQUESTS NIMROD CONTEMPLATED
   A. A One-World Sovereignty
   B. A One-World Society
   C. A One-World Sanctuary

---

There are approximately 5,687 languages in the world. As anyone who has traveled in a foreign country knows, nothing contributes as much to the separation of the nations as the almost insurmountable language barrier. God's original intention was that the various tribal families should migrate and settle in different areas. Nimrod, whose name means "rebel," urged people to ignore God's wise plan and dreamed of a centralized superstate with himself as its superman. He was the prime mover behind the building of the tower of Babel. God used the confusion of tongues to defeat Nimrod's soaring ambitions and to accomplish His original purpose for the human race.

The name *Nimrod* had become a byword by the time of Moses. Its numerical significance is worth considering. Every letter of the Hebrew alphabet is also a number. Thus every word has a numerical value. The sum of the numerical values of the letters in *Nimrod* is 294, or 7 times 42. The number 42, like the number 666, is associated with the antichrist.[1] The first part of the antichrist's career, during which he will rise to world domination, will last for 42 months. The second part of his career, which will culminate in his swift and certain fall, will also last for 42 months. In Scripture the number 7 stands for perfection. Since the perfect number is linked with the antichrist's number in the name *Nimrod,* we understand that the man Nimrod was not just a type of the antichrist; he was a perfect type of the antichrist.

# I. THE CONNECTIONS NIMROD CULTIVATED

Nimrod was the grandson of Ham, the progenitor of several African peoples. Every major invention that made civilization possible was developed by a descendant of Ham. Westerners often overlook that historical fact. The great Egyptian empire was Hamitic. Enormous contributions to the world's knowledge were made by the Egyptians and they had extraordinary farming and engineering skills. Their pyramids rank among the seven wonders of the ancient world and their warriors were famous for their effective use of fast-moving war chariots in battle.

However, Egyptian civilization, for all its flair and flourish, was a mere sideshow. It is not even mentioned in the early chapters of Genesis. It is represented only by Mizraim, whose achievements are passed over in silence. It was Nimrod who immediately leaped to fame.

Nimrod cultivated his connections with his grandfather Ham and his granduncles Shem and Japheth. What stories these men had to tell to a bright boy who was eager to learn and hungry for power!

We can easily picture Nimrod asking Ham a host of questions. "Tell me, Grandpa, what was the world like when you were a boy?"

And we can imagine how Ham answered his grandson. "What I recall most vividly, Nimrod, were the people. The world was filled with people. They built great cities and filled them with works of art and the products of science and industry. That was really Cain's idea. He had a mark on him and people were afraid of him. But he wanted to have lots of people around him, so he invented city life as a means to bring people together." Little Nimrod's eyes no doubt grew wide with wonder. *Cities!* he thought. *Great cities!* He liked that idea.

"And there was music," we can hear Ham saying. "The world was filled with all kinds of music. There was music for the harp and music for the pipes. There was beat and rhythm and swelling volumes of vibrant sound. Men marched to music; women danced to music; people sang to music. When I was a boy, the world was wonderful. It was a world of entertainment.

"And it was a world of science, Nimrod. People knew how to build things and invent things. We knew so much! Our father Adam had eaten of the tree of knowledge, and the world was filled with the fruit of our knowledge. We developed agriculture and found new ways to herd cattle. We evolved new methods of marketing. We made great strides in metallurgy and smelting. We learned how to make things—big things like the ark."

We can also imagine Nimrod talking to his granduncle Japheth, who was much more approachable than austere, spiritual Shem. "What was the world like, Uncle Japheth, when you were a boy?"

"Ah, Nimrod," Japheth might have said, "when I was a boy like you, the world was very wicked. It was full of vice and violence. I well recall the moral pollution and the godlessness of those days. People forgot all about God and His word. They were really secular humanists who thought only of this world. In the end God had to send the flood."

"Oh!" Nimrod surely exclaimed. "Tell me about the flood. You were in the ark. Tell me all about that."

We can hear Japheth saying, "My brothers and I helped

our father Noah build the ark. It was hard work. We had to fell giant trees and lay a massive keel. It took us 120 years to build that boat. People who came to see it stared in astonishment. Some of them mocked us. Some went away shaking their heads. My father preached to them and warned them to flee from the wrath to come. We made hundreds of rooms inside the ark and covered the whole outside with pitch.

"When it was finished, Methuselah died. He was my great-grandfather, the son of godly Enoch who was raptured home to Heaven. After we buried Methuselah, we went into the ark. And nothing happened! For a week we were the laughingstock of the whole world. It was the longest, hardest week of my life. I can still remember how those foolish people made fun of us. Then God suddenly closed the door and the rains came. Pray to God, Nimrod, that you never see God's wrath outpoured like that."

In Nimrod's day the memory of the flood was still very much alive. If anyone was inclined to forget, old Shem—the supreme patriarch under Noah—no doubt quickly reminded him. Although Shem was the youngest of Noah's sons, by divine appointment he wielded the spiritual power in the new world. It was Shem who reminded people of the Lord's coming and kept alive the vital truths of the early chapters of Genesis.

Japheth talked and Nimrod listened eagerly and thought deeply, but he was most impressed with Ham and his secret plans for a new humanistic society. Nimrod longed to be free and to set people free from the irritating religious restrictions that noble-minded Shem imposed on the world. Religion might have a place in Nimrod's ambitious plans, but not Shem's kind of religion. Nimrod wanted no part in a system of beliefs that was connected with the mighty name of the promised Savior of the world.

Nimrod probably cultivated the friendship of Uncle Canaan in spite of warnings to stay away from him. Canaan lived under Noah's divinely-inspired curse, yet somehow he seemed to prosper. He even had his own religion. But that religion would become so vile that God would have to command Joshua to exterminate the whole Canaanite race.

Nimrod found a kindred soul in Canaan. We can imagine the young rebel asking about the curse. "What happened, Uncle Canaan?"

"Never you mind, you rascal," we can almost hear Canaan say.

"But doesn't being under a curse make you afraid?"

"Me? I don't put any stock in that kind of talk. What harm has it done me? I don't think I'm cursed. I think I'm blessed. Look at all the sons I have."

Nimrod would think of his tough-minded, rambunctious cousins. Sidon, Canaan's firstborn would be the forebear of the Phoenician seafarers. Their great ships and mighty cities would dominate the world for years. Jebus would one day found the city of Jerusalem and the descendants of another cousin would become the imperial Amorites, whose wickedness would be proverbial in Abraham's day.

Nimrod continued to cultivate his connections with Ham and Canaan. It didn't matter to him that God had saved his grandfather from the flood. Nimrod was not impressed with his family's account of salvation through the grace of God from the outpoured wrath of God. The truth of salvation through the shed blood of the lamb was known and taught in his day, but he was not interested. Nimrod did not want that kind of religion. He rebelled against the gospel. *It's for old women and children*, he probably thought. *It's not for me. If I have my way, I will liberate people from all that. I will convert the remains of the ark on mount Ararat into a museum of antiquities so that people can study the science and technology of a former age.*

## II. THE CONQUESTS NIMROD CONTEMPLATED

Daring plans seethed in Nimrod's mind. He was plotting nothing less than the conquest of the world. God had placed the sword of the magistrate into Noah's hands and commanded that murderers be executed: "Whoso sheddeth man's blood, by man shall his blood be shed" (Genesis 9:6). Nimrod planned to take the magistrate's sword and transform it into a conqueror's sword. He would use it to execute anyone who got in his way.

But first he had to prove himself and win the admiration, respect, and gratitude of everyone. Also he needed to perfect his skill in the use of weapons, invent new weapons, and develop imaginative ways to use them. *The best way for me to accomplish all these goals,* he doubtless reasoned, *is to become a hunter. By doing so, I will become a benefactor to mankind. Dangerous animals are multiplying and if I can rid the world of ferocious beasts, I will be hailed by one and all. I can develop my courage and proficiency at the same time. Moreover I will attract a band of brave, determined men who will accept my leadership and become the nucleus of an army.*

Nimrod implemented his novel ideas. He became a hunter and eventually a hero. Then, like the conquerors who followed, he became a hunter of men. He was the first of many who initially posed as benefactors and then became tyrants.

Although the Bible does not go into all the details, it lets us see the shadowy figure of this great rebel and renowned hunter looming over the building of Babel. Scripture also lets us see a glimpse of him founding two of the most important population centers of the ancient world: Nineveh and Babylon.[2] Both the Assyrian and Babylonian empires had their roots in Nimrod's enterprise.

Nimrod seems to have been infuriated by the lack of blessedness that marked the family of Ham. God had blessed Shem and had promised that the Messiah would come from among his descendants.[3] God had also blessed Japheth and had promised to "enlarge" him (Genesis 9:27). Great imperial nations would spring from him. Moreover Japheth's descendants would share the spiritual blessings associated with the Shemitic race. But God had neither blessed nor cursed Ham. He was ignored as if he did not exist. For Ham there was nothing, but for his son Canaan there was a curse.

Filled with resentment over God's treatment of his family, Nimrod determined to reverse the blessings and the curse. He would build a city and an empire in which a new world religion would find its home. He would defy God and not allow the peoples of the earth to be scattered. He would shepherd them, unite them, and control them. He would build a one-world sovereignty, a one-world society, and a one-world sanctuary. He would prove Noah to be a false prophet and Shem's God to be futile.

## A. A One-World Sovereignty

Nimrod wanted Babylon—the city he would build—to become the capital of the world and the focal point of all science, art, and industry. That city would rule the world and he would rule that city.

God, however, was not impressed with his plans. The Holy Spirit contemptuously commented, "They had brick for stone, and slime had they for morter" (Genesis 11:3). When God builds, He builds with stone—He builds for eternity. The end-time empire of the antichrist (of which Nimrod's empire was the first foreshadowing on earth) will be destroyed by a stone. That stone, cut without hands, will become a great mountain and fill the whole earth (Daniel 2:31-45).

Nimrod built with brick. Brick, which is hard-baked clay, is like fallen man, who is set in his ways of rebellion against God. And Nimrod chose to use slime for mortar. So his proposed world empire was symbolized by hard-baked clay and slime. The clay represented the intrinsic weakness of his kingdom and the slime its intentional wickedness.

Some day another rebel will build another empire of brick. The Bible calls him the beast, the man of sin. Humanism will be his philosophy; fallen men, hardened in sin, will be his building blocks; and sin will be the cement he uses to bind the world together. He too will establish a capital—in Nimrod's old Babylon, now known as Iraq. It will be a Vanity Fair, a "cage of every unclean and hateful bird" (Revelation 18:2). Iraq's ambitions to dominate the Middle East will only be realized when it joins forces with the antichrist, who will rebuild the ancient city of Babylon and make it the economic center of the world. Its catastrophic destruction will be as sure as that of Nimrod's capital, and far more spectacular.

## B. A One-World Society

"And the whole earth," Scripture records, "was of one language, and of one speech" (Genesis 11:1). Nothing is more frustrating to those who espouse a one-world philosophy than the language barrier. Nothing shuts a man off from his fellows more completely than the inability to communicate.

I have sat through church services that were conducted in Spanish, German, Norwegian, and Italian and have watched with a certain degree of envy as everyone else enjoyed the meetings while I was unable to understand what was being said. Other people occasionally nodded their heads in agreement with the speakers, now and then shook their heads sadly, and once in a while burst into sudden roars of laughter, but I might just as well have stayed at home. I sat among the congregation, but apart from them. When I returned to a society where everyone spoke English, I felt as if I were stepping out of darkness into light.

Today the English language is rapidly assuming the status of a world language. Nearly everyone in Europe speaks English. When India gained its independence from Britain, it found out how useful English is. The new republic tried to make Hindi its official language, but had little success. India has some 179 languages, so it has to rely on English to unify it.

The sun never sets on the English language. More than 400 million people speak it. It has replaced French as the language of diplomacy and German as the language of science. English is the official language of thousands of international societies and more than 80 percent of all scientific papers are published first in English. It is the dominant language in the fields of medicine, electronics, space technology, aviation, international business, advertising, radio, television, and film. Thus people who do not know English are culturally, economically, and scientifically deprived. In today's world a knowledge of English is not merely valuable; it is essential.

Whether or not the antichrist will impose English on the world as the language of his empire remains to be seen. It is possible of course that he will introduce some new technology capable of overcoming language barriers.

The universal language of Nimrod's day must have been a tremendous vehicle for uniting mankind. Ideas could be exchanged freely, smoothly, and swiftly. Technology, science, business, and society took on a universal character. Mind control was easy. The common language was an invaluable tool for disseminating Nimrod's ideas and promoting his ambitious plans for a one-world society.

## C. A One-World Sanctuary

Nimrod's proposed world religion would center in a tower "whose top may reach unto heaven" (Genesis 11:4). A better translation might be "a tower and its top with the heavens." The tower was to have a zodiac on its top, and astrology—along with the fortunetelling and occultism that accompany it—was to be the common religion. A new age was to be inaugurated. Daring new ideas were to replace the scorned doctrines upheld by Shem.

Humanism was the basic philosophy of Nimrod and his followers. They sought to depose God and enthrone man. "Let us make *us* a name," they said (italics added).

There is more to this statement than meets the eye. The name *Shem* literally means "the name." Through Shem's lineage would come the Christ, the One with the saving, sanctifying, sovereign name. Noah said, "Blessed be the Lord God of Shem" (Genesis 9:26). We could make a substitution and read, "Blessed be the Lord God of the name." Shem was the custodian of God's true salvation that was forever identified by God with "the name."

We read about that name in key verses of the New Testament. Matthew 1:21 says, "Thou shalt call his *name* JESUS: for he shall save his people from their sins." Acts 4:12 says, "Neither is there salvation in any other: for there is none other *name* under heaven given among men, whereby we must be saved." Paul wrote in Philippians 2:9-10, "God also hath...given him a *name* which is above every name: That at the *name* of Jesus every knee should bow" (italics added).

Satan hates that name and fears it. It is the name that commands the Father's heart in Heaven, the name that opens the gates of glory, the name that can bind Satan and cast out evil spirits.

Those old-time empire-builders thought they knew a better name. They wanted to depose Shem and all that he stood for in terms of God's truth. They wanted to establish a new religion and hail the name of Nimrod.

Jesus said to the Jews of His day, "I am come in my Father's name, and ye receive me not: if another shall come in his own name, him ye will receive" (John 5:43). This statement is a clear reference to the antichrist, who will come "in his own name." This rebel will gather a wondering world around the focal point of his mystical name, which will be recognized by the number 666 (Revelation 13:17-18). The name of the antichrist will be a clear forgery of the name of Jesus. The numerical value of the antichrist's name stands in deliberate, defiant contrast to the numerical value of the name of Jesus (888).[4]

Nimrod's goal was to build a federation of nations and exclude the true God from the new world order. He embarked on this ambitious project boldly enough, but he accomplished nothing lasting. God simply stepped in and destroyed the whole scheme by confounding human speech.

We do not know what happened to Nimrod in the end. Perhaps he was executed by Shem. A great deal of research has gone into the mystery of his death and into the legends that grew up around him. He seems to have become, posthumously, the mystical head of a new apostate religion, which depicted him as a child in the arms of his mother. According to Alexander Hislop, Nimrod and his wife Semiramis invented idolatry.[5] Belief in the elaborate Babylonian mysteries spread and tainted the thinking of all mankind. They still influence scores of religions, including that of Rome.

Some time ago I came out of the Atlanta airport and boarded a bus that I thought was headed for the Windy Hill terminal near Marietta. I began reading a book to pass the time. Presently I looked out of the window and noticed that we were not passing the usual landmarks. For a few minutes I was totally confused, but then I realized I had boarded the wrong bus! I was headed for the Radisson Inn instead of the Windy Hill terminal. It was a simple but costly mistake. I would have to go back to the airport and start all over again or take a cab from the Radisson Inn to my home. I decided to take a cab, and it cost me a great deal of money.

Many people make an even costlier mistake when they are faced with choosing one of two roads that run through life. One road begins with Seth, passes through Golgotha, and leads to the heavenly Jerusalem. The other begins with Cain, passes through Babel, and leads to the lake of fire. We were born on the broad road that leads to destruction. We need to get off that road by coming to Calvary. From there we can start our journey to Heaven. Nimrod chose to stay on the broad road. He enjoyed a few years of cheering and applause, and then the darkness of death overtook him. Now he is in that "blackness of darkness for ever" (Jude 13). He has been in a lost eternity for thousands of years, yet his anguish and remorse have hardly begun.

1. See Daniel 9:27 and appendix 90 in *The Companion Bible*.
2. See Genesis 10:8-12. Also see Alexander Hislop, *The Two Babylons* (Neptune, NJ: Loizeaux, 1959).

# 4
# Abraham
# and His God

*Hebrews 11:8-19*

---

I. GOD DISCOVERS HIS MAN

II. GOD DETACHES HIS MAN

III. GOD DEVELOPS HIS MAN

    A. Blessing

    B. Betrayal

    C. Barrenness

    D. Brethren

    E. Backsliding

IV. GOD DISPLAYS HIS MAN

---

Years ago when I was in Bethlehem, I found my way to a local gathering of believers on a Sunday morning. There I met a potter who invited me to come to see his workshop. I accepted his invitation and during my visit learned about the process of making pottery in the Holy Land.

First the potter *discovers* his clay. He locates a field that yields the kind of clay he wants to use in producing his earthenware.

Then he purchases the field and removes some manageable pieces of clay, which he takes into his shop. From these pieces he *detaches* smaller lumps, sized for whichever vessel he intends to make.

Next he *develops* his clay. He begins to squeeze the lump between his fingers and pound it with his fist in order to soften the clay and make it malleable. It is of no use to him as long as it is stiff and unyielding. If he detects any impurities, he removes them so that they will not spoil the finished product.

Then he places the developed clay on the center of his wheel. The wheel is not elaborate—just a flat circular surface with a spindle that runs down to another wheel. The potter turns the lower wheel with his feet, causing the upper wheel on which the clay reposes to revolve. Round and round it goes, spinning dizzily. The potter moistens his hands and begins to apply pressure to the sides of the lump of clay. As he does, the clay begins to change shape. It grows taller and taller, becoming a rotating cylinder. The potter moistens his hands again and, using his thumb, puts pressure on the top of the cylinder. Soon a hollow is formed. He puts his hands in the hollow and as he applies more and more pressure on the inside of the cylinder, the lump of clay begins to take on beauty and form.

At last a shapely vase is ready. But the potter is not through. He places the vase into a primitive oven and proceeds to stoke the fire. The vase remains in that oven for many hours, during which the potter watches the temperature with an eagle eye. When the fire has finished its work, the potter removes from the furnace a vessel of usefulness and grace.

He then *displays* the vase with his other wares on a shelf outside his workshop. There in the bright sunshine his creations stand, waiting to be purchased and put to work. Each piece is a tribute to the skill of the potter.

This process illustrates perfectly the story of Abraham. It also mirrors the story of every born-again child of God. God discovers His man, detaches him, develops him, and then displays him. Let us follow this process in the life of Abraham.

# I. GOD DISCOVERS HIS MAN

God knows all about us. He knows our names and our addresses. He knows our parents, our relatives, and our friends. He knows where we were born, where we went to school, where we work, how long we have worked there, what we do, and how much money we earn. He knows what time we get up in the morning and when we get home at night. And He knew exactly where to discover Abraham.

Abraham lived in Ur of the Chaldees, an important center of moon worship on the great Euphrates river. Like all of his neighbors, Abraham was a lost idolatrous pagan, but he had an illustrious family tree. He could trace his ancestry back to Shem, Noah, Seth, and Adam and Eve. Some outstanding patriarchs and prophets were among his forebears, but the memory of that glorious past had become murky in the folklore of his race. Abraham may have forgotten his ancestry, but God had not forgotten it. And when God went looking for a man, He looked among the descendants of Shem.

As always, God took the initiative. Out of the depths of His great heart of love, God spoke to the depths of Abraham's empty, yearning heart. He spoke to Abraham because that is His way. The Bible says that "faith cometh by hearing, and hearing by the word of God" (Romans 10:17).

God spoke to Abraham about another country. The Epistle to the Hebrews tells us that when Abraham set forth on his pilgrimage, he looked for "a city which hath foundations, whose builder and maker is God" (Hebrews 11:10). That unknown city haunted Abraham's dreams. He did not find it in the great population centers of Babylon, along the fertile crescent, in the Jordan valley, or along the banks of the Nile.

Indeed we have to read all the way through the Bible, from Genesis to Revelation, before we finally find that city "which hath foundations." And when we find it, we see that it has twelve foundations ablaze with precious stones! (Revelation 21:14,19) That city, located somewhere beyond the confines of space and in another time dimension, awaits the day when, at the second coming of Christ, it will be revealed to everyone who dwells on the earth (Revelation 21:10).

God speaks about that city to everyone who has an ear to hear. Jesus came from that city, where the streets are paved with gold, the walls are made of jasper, and the gates are created out of pearl. Through that city flows the crystal stream and the tree of life grows along its banks. That city has no need of sun or moon because Jesus fills it with His light. Sorrow, death, and pain are unknown there. Bright angels are that city's ministers and the saints of God its citizens. Its glorious King once wore a crown of thorns, but now He is crowned with glory. He rules galactic empires whose vastness is beyond the scope of puny human thought.

God gave sinful Abraham a passport to that city the moment he took Him at His word and exercised faith in that word. By faith Abraham became a citizen. We too can become citizens by faith. Otherwise the city's gates are bolted and its glories are barred to us.

## II. GOD DETACHES HIS MAN

God's first demand on Abraham's faith was obedience, because obedience activates faith. Obedience proves that our belief is genuine, saving, living faith.

God had told Abraham to leave his home and become a pilgrim and a stranger on the earth. He was to turn his back on what was familiar and live by faith, not by sight. Moreover he was never to return to his old way of life.

The call to salvation is always followed by the call to separation. That is why God, after He created light, "divided the light from the darkness" (Genesis 1:3-4). Paul asked, "What communion hath light with darkness?...What part hath he that believeth with an infidel? And what agreement hath the temple of God with idols?" (2 Corinthians 6:14-16) The answer of course is "None!" God separated the light from the darkness; He separated the waters above the firmament from the waters below the firmament; He separated the land from the sea. Separation is one of the major doctrinal themes underlying Genesis 1. Abraham obeyed the call to separation.

We can picture him one bright sunny morning entering the First National Bank of Babylon to close his account. And we can imagine the panic on the premises when he announces his intention. I used to work for a large bank and I know what happens when the richest man in town comes in. The red carpet is rolled out! He is ushered into the manager's office with due deference, seated in the most comfortable chair, and regaled with freshly brewed coffee. Then the manager asks his opinion about the state of the economy and the latest bargain on the stock market. Perhaps the Babylonian banker's conversation with Abraham went something like this:

"Good morning, sir. So good to see you. What can I do for you?"

"I've come to close my account. I'll take it all in cash, please. Gold coins or gold bars will do."

We can almost see the bank manager collapse on the spot. He sinks weakly into his chair behind his desk of polished oak and stares at his visitor. "Close your account?" he whispers. He has visions of a furious head office demanding his instant resignation. "But Mr. Abraham, why?" he finally asks. "What have we done to displease you?"

"Nothing. I'm selling out and leaving town."

The bank manager does not want to give up without a struggle so he tries another angle. "Can we transfer your account? We have branches all over Babylonia."

"No, thank you. I'm leaving the country. I'm going abroad."

"Can we transfer your account to one of our affiliate banks? We have correspondents all over the crescent."

"No, thank you. I'll take it all in cash. I have ten camels outside. You can put the money in goatskin bags and my men will load them on the camels."

"But where are you going, Mr. Abraham? I'm sure we can be of service to you wherever you go. What about letters of credit? Our name is good from here to Egypt. Where are you going, sir?"

"I haven't the faintest idea!"

"I beg your pardon?"

"I haven't any idea where I'm going."

"You haven't any idea? You're leaving town, closing your account, and going abroad, and you don't know where you're going?"

"That's right. So I'll take my money in cash."

"But…"

"No, Mr. Manager, I'm not crazy. I don't know where I'm going, but God does. You see, the other day God spoke to me—the God who created the stars and the seas. He told me to leave my country and go to another one. I think He was talking about Heaven because He spoke of a city whose builder and maker is God. I haven't any idea where it is. All I know is that it's not here. To get to it I have to obey God and become a pilgrim and a stranger on the earth. So I'll take my money in cash. I don't know if I can take it with me, but I'm certainly not leaving it here."

We can well imagine the kind of report that the distraught bank manager sent to his head office that night:

> I regret to inform you that Abraham of Ur came into the bank this morning and withdrew all his holdings in gold bullion. He refused to transfer his account to another branch. He refused a letter of credit. Believe it or not, he said that he had heard from Heaven, and God had told him to become a pilgrim. He is leaving town permanently and since he has no idea where he is going or what he will be doing, he closed his account.

Up till now Abraham has been one of the sanest men I know and one of the most successful businessmen in Babylon, but evidently he has succumbed to religious mania. There was no reasoning with him.

Thus Abraham put feet to his faith. He became a pilgrim and a stranger as far as this world was concerned. As a stranger, Abraham was *away* from home; as a pilgrim, he was *going* home. Thenceforth he could say:

This world is not my home, I'm just a passing thru,
My treasures are laid up somewhere beyond the blue.[1]

God had detached His man. Abraham would not have been useful to God if he had remained wedded to this world. Because he translated his faith into obedience, Abraham became a great man in the household of faith.

## III. GOD DEVELOPS HIS MAN

God brought all kinds of experiences into Abraham's life to develop His man. Sometimes Abraham enjoyed mountaintop experiences. Other times he walked through dark valleys of despair. Sometimes he savored victory. Other times he tasted defeat. Whether his experiences brought sunshine or shadow, glorious faith or miserable doubt, they all became grist in God's mill. Chapter after chapter, Abraham's story reveals how God mellowed him and matured him.

### A. Blessing

God told Abraham, "I will bless thee" (Genesis 12:2). The Old Testament word translated "bless" carries with it the idea of happiness. Since the word is invariably in the plural, the sentence means, "I will make you a happy, happy man."

So Abraham traveled to the land where God had promised to bless him and built his first altar at *Bethel,* which means "the house of God." But then he made two discoveries: there was a famine in the land, and the land was inhabited by the foe. Abraham did not expect to encounter such obstacles. He needed to learn that in the place where God's people find their blessings, they also find their battles. The same lesson is taught on the spiritual level in the book of Ephesians.

## B. Betrayal

Suddenly Egypt looked attractive to the disillusioned pilgrim. Surely he could not stay in Canaan under the conditions he found. Egypt, however, was just another form of Babylon, the world in another guise. By *the world* I mean human life and society with God left out. It is the devil's lair for sinners and his lure for saints.

As Abraham's heart gravitated toward Egypt, he found himself suggesting to Sarah that they lay the foundation of their future on a falsehood (Genesis 12:10-20). Consequently the world made a coward and a liar out of him. He lost his testimony in Egypt. Instead of being a blessing to the pharaoh, Abraham became a curse to him. The couple were covered with shame and confusion and in the end the pharaoh drove them out. As Abraham and Sarah stole away, they may well have overheard the pharaoh saying to his courtiers, "Well, if he's an example of a believer, I hope I never meet another one."

## C. Barrenness

God had promised Abraham seed as numerous as the stars of heaven (Genesis 15:5). But when years went by with no prospect of a son, Abraham decided to take matters into his own hands and help God out. He resorted to a worldly and carnal expedient, marrying Sarah's Egyptian slave girl Hagar, by whom he had a son. As a result God did not speak to Abraham for thirteen years. (In the Bible the number thirteen is associated with rebellion.)

Abraham had to learn that the answer to barrenness is not to be found in worldly expedients. Many churches need to learn the same lesson today. When a church is barren, it does no lasting good to resort to bigger budgets, better music, more eloquent preaching, and more sophisticated advertising. The answer is to be found in God alone. Barren spells as well as showers of blessing are often needful in the spiritual development of a congregation.

## D. Brethren

Abraham had many trials because of his nephew Lot, who had a secondhand faith. We know that Lot was a believer because the Holy Spirit calls him "righteous" and thus puts him on a par with Abraham (2 Peter 2:7-8). But Lot spent much of his time backsliding. Like Demas (see 2 Timothy 4:10), he loved this present evil world.

At great personal risk Abraham made a valiant attempt to restore backslidden Lot to the fellowship of the people of God (Genesis 14), but Lot returned to Sodom. He said in effect, "Thank you very much, Uncle Abraham, but this pilgrim life is not for me. My place is in Sodom. Indeed the king of Sodom has offered me a very attractive position. My fortune is made! And I am to have a say in the government of Sodom, so I will be able to use my influence to help stem the tide of wickedness. Sodom is my mission field."

But plans like Lot's never work. If a person wants to lift a barrel, he must first get out of it. If he wants to raise the world, he must first find a lever that is long enough and a fulcrum that is far enough away.

In the end Abraham, the separated man, had a greater impact on his and future generations than Lot, who fraternized with the filthy legislators of Sodom.

## E. Backsliding

After his disastrous experience in Egypt, Abraham must have said to himself, *Never again! I've learned my lesson.* But he hadn't. He repeated the whole wretched cycle with Abimelech, the king of the Philistines (Genesis 20).

God had to teach Abraham, who was "the father of all them that believe" (Romans 4:11), that the heart of man, even the heart of a believing man, is "deceitful above all things, and desperately wicked" (Jeremiah 17:9). There is no sin that a genuine believer cannot commit except blasphemy against the Holy Ghost. Within his heart is a volcano that can erupt at any time.

So the aging patriarch had his ups and downs until at last he earned the lovely title, "the Friend of God" (James 2:23; also see 2 Chronicles 20:7 and Isaiah 41:8). God has few friends. He has countless millions of servants. Among them are the shining seraphim, the chanting cherubim, and angels and archangels without number, who hang on His words and rush to do His bidding. God has many children as well. Through the exceeding riches of His grace, every blood-bought child of Adam's ruined race who has been ransomed, healed, restored, forgiven, and indwelt and baptized by the Holy Spirit is a child of God. But it is possible to have a child and still not have a friend.

A child can be rebellious and wayward, riding roughshod over everything his parents hold dear. In such a case there is no basis for fellowship unless the child gets saved. Then his life is made new in Christ, he comes back to God, he takes his rightful place with his parents in the house of God, and establishes a friendship with his parents.

God wants friends. He does not have many friends on earth, but Abraham was one of those rare individuals. As he pursued his way through life, he sought to do what would please the living and true God. We can imagine God looking down benevolently on Abraham and saying to Gabriel, Michael, and the angels, "Do you see that elderly man down there? He's my friend." Again and again God would visit Abraham. Once He brought two angels with Him and they stopped by Abraham's place and shared a meal with him (Genesis 18:1-8).

Jesus has taught us what we must do to become friends of God. The formula is simple; anyone can qualify. "Ye are my friends," Jesus said, "if ye do whatsoever I command you" (John 15:14).

# IV. GOD DISPLAYS HIS MAN

"And it came to pass after these things, that God did tempt Abraham.... And he said, Take now thy son...into the land of Moriah; and offer him there for a burnt offering upon one of the mountains which I will tell thee of" (Genesis 22:1-2). God arranged this scene in order to put His man on display. He wanted to show the world what Calvary was like from the standpoint of God the Father.

We often think of what Calvary meant to God the Son, but we seldom think of what Calvary meant to God the Father. Many of our hymns about Calvary tell of the suffering of the Son, but few of them describe how the cross touched the heart of the Father. In effect God said to Abraham, "To show the world what it means for me as a heavenly Father to take My only begotten Son to a place called Calvary, I want you as a human father to take your only begotten son[2] to a place called mount Moriah."

Ever since then, whenever anyone wants to know how Calvary touched the heart of the Father, all he has to do is read the magnificent story recorded in Genesis 22. Each time we read it, we see the father and the son journeying together to that terrible hill of pain, we feel Abraham's anguish as he takes his knife to slay his son, and we understand to some degree the anguish Calvary brought to God the Father.

God puts us through the same process today. He discovers us, detaches us, and develops us so that He might display us. He wants us to be the prime exhibit of His grace for time and eternity. As Paul wrote:

> God, who is rich in mercy, for his great love wherewith he loved us, Even when we were dead in sins, hath

quickened us together with Christ...And hath raised us up together, and made us sit together in heavenly places in Christ Jesus: That in the ages to come he might shew the exceeding riches of his grace in his kindness toward us through Christ Jesus (Ephesians 2:4-7).

God is going to show to an admiring universe the amazing skillfulness of His hands in taking the unpromising clay of Adam's race and transforming it into vessels of beauty, glory, and eternal usefulness. "Hallelujah, what a Savior!"[3]

---

1. From the hymn "This World Is Not My Home," arranged by Albert E. Brumley.
2. See Hebrews 11:17.
3. From the hymn "Hallelujah, What a Savior!" by Philip P. Bliss.

# 5
# Job
# and His Redeemer

*Job 19:23-27*

---

I. THE REDEMPTION OF CHRIST
II. THE RESURRECTION OF CHRIST
III. THE RETURN OF CHRIST
IV. THE RELATIONSHIP OF CHRIST

---

P oor old Job! He had lost his family, his fortune, and his health, and his wife had turned against him. In the little cemetery behind his house lay the mortal remains of all ten of his children. Bankruptcy stared him in the face and with varying degrees of harshness his so-called friends looked at him askance, accusing him of being a sinner and a hypocrite.

Disaster after disaster had swept over Job and he had no idea why these calamities had overtaken him. As far as he knew, he had always sought to honor God. He had kept himself from impurity, from indifference to the needs of others, and from pride. He had lived a good, moral, God-fearing life.

As he writhed in agony of body and soul, those who knew him gathered around to rub salt into his wounds. Job vacillated from anger to anguish to assurance. Sometimes his faith faltered; sometimes it flamed, as in Job 19:25. In desperation, yet with determination, he took hold of God. "I *know*," he said, "that my redeemer liveth" (italics added). At that point he could have sung the old hymn we have come to love:

> Blessed assurance, Jesus is mine!
> O what a foretaste of glory divine!
> Heir of salvation, purchase of God,
> Born of His Spirit, washed in His blood.[1]

Nothing that the world has to offer can compare with this assurance. In the wake of a catastrophe, the unsaved man is helpless and often hopeless. The best his friends can say is, "We're sorry! That's too bad! We hope your luck changes soon." Or they may say, even more fatuously, "Everything is going to be all right." The only person who really knows that everything is going to be all right is the blood-bought child of God.

Faced with adversity, Job simply cast his anchor inside the veil (Hebrews 6:19). The storm tides rose and the cables strained, but the anchor held fast.

"I know that my redeemer liveth," Job said. He wanted these words to be *preserved:* "Oh that my words were now written!" (Job 19:23) The spoken word can so easily be forgotten, distorted, or wrenched out of context. So Job wanted his words to be put in writing.

He also wanted his words to be *published:* "Oh that they were printed in a book!" He wanted his words to be circulated as widely as possible, to be spread abroad until they reached the ends of the earth.

Finally he wanted his words to be *perpetuated:* "[Oh] that they were graven with an iron pen and lead in the rock for ever!" Job hoped that all the generations to come would grasp what he had to say.

God granted Job's request. He immortalized Job's words in the Word of God. The sun, moon, stars, mountains, rocks, and hills will all pass away, but Job's words, embedded in the Word of God, will last forever.

Let us consider Job's immortal statement, wrung from the lips of a man whose heart had been broken by one misfortune after another, by death after death, by disagreement after disagreement, and by delay after delay. His words reveal something about the redemption of Christ, the resurrection of Christ, the return of Christ, and the relationship of Christ.

# I. THE REDEMPTION OF CHRIST

When Job said, "I know that my redeemer liveth," the great Biblical truths concerning the Redeemer were as yet unpublished. Job did not have a single page of Scripture to instruct him. All he had was the knowledge of the sacred traditions that had been handed down in his family from time immemorial from father to son. As far as we know, Exodus and Ruth, the two books in the Old Testament that pre-eminently set forth the concept of redemption, had not yet been penned.

The book of Exodus dramatically portrays redemption by power. God set the stage in a major world power, cast Moses and the pharaoh in the leading roles, and used three to four million Hebrew slaves as the supporting cast. The exodus from Egypt was an enactment, on the grandest scale in all history, of the principle of liberation from sin.

In the Bible, Egypt often symbolizes the world in which we live, a world that is settled in its hostility toward God. Egypt, like our world, was magnificent in its own way, but its principles, policies, pleasures, pursuits, prosperity, and power were diametrically opposed to God.

In the drama of the exodus, the pharaoh—Egypt's prince— represents the "prince of this world," the evil one with all his antagonism toward God's people and God's purposes. The Jews—born into slavery, living under the sentence of death, and groaning in misery and bondage—represent the earth's lost souls. Moses, the kinsman-redeemer, represents the Savior, the One sent from God to set those sinners free.

There was no way the enslaved Hebrews could free

themselves. Their case was hopeless apart from God. For them redemption needed to be by might. Pharaoh had to be subdued and his kingdom wrenched from him. He had to be left shattered, empty, and defeated by a power far greater than his own. So God armed Moses with divine power and he performed a series of spectacular miracles that laid Egypt in the dust.

Finally the Passover lamb was slain—its blood was shed. The people of God chose to find shelter behind that blood and then God's redemption went into effect. The ransomed Hebrews marched in triumph out of Egypt.

God had demonstrated redemption by power. He redeems His people by using His irresistible might to break Satan's grasp and set his slaves free forever.

The book of Ruth portrays redemption by purchase. Ruth, as a Moabitess, was alienated from God and under the curse of the law. She was a lost pagan—without God, without Christ, and without hope.

Ruth married into a Jewish family, but soon became a widow. Hebrew law required the brother of the deceased to marry the widow and raise a family in his brother's name. He also had to purchase any of his brother's property that had fallen into other hands. This provision would be especially important in a situation such as Ruth's in which the property might have passed into the hands of foreigners. Under the land laws of Israel all property had to remain in the family to which it was originally deeded by God.

When Ruth, the Moabite widow of a Hebrew landowner, arrived in Bethlehem with her mother-in-law Naomi, those laws went into effect. Ruth was a widow indeed, having been bereft of husband and brother-in-law alike, so a relative named Boaz, "a mighty man of wealth," purchased both her person and her property. Thus she who was outlawed from God was brought into the family of God. Her story illustrates redemption by purchase.

Jesus became our kinsman-redeemer so that we who by

birth and circumstance were alienated from God could be united to Him by faith. On the cross Jesus, that mighty man of wealth, paid the price of our redemption, not with mere silver and gold but with His precious blood.

He bought us! We belong to Him! Through the salvation Christ offers, we can be united to Him just as Ruth was united to Boaz. Christ redeemed our property as well. He secured the right and title to the world in which we live.

Both Exodus and Ruth point forward, down through the centuries, to Christ, who would redeem us by power and by purchase. Job, however, knew nothing about the development of the concept of redemption in the Old Testament. He only knew that He needed a Redeemer and that God had provided such a Redeemer. Job was speaking of the redemption Christ would bring when he said, "I know...my redeemer!"

# II. THE RESURRECTION OF CHRIST

The whole Bible testifies that Christ purchased our redemption by dying on the cross of Calvary. Every Old Testament sacrifice mirrored that coming redemption.

A dreadful finality robes death with terrors and torments. A body in a casket indicates the end of physical life, the severing of human ties. Medical science has no power to raise the dead. Human love is not strong enough. We can call and curse, coax and caress, command and cry, but the dead person pays no heed.

It seemed that the end had come when Jesus died on the cross. His enemies had done their worst and exhausted their malice. After the soldier plunged his spear into the Lord's side, His body was taken down by loving hands. Joseph of Arimathaea provided a new tomb and Nicodemus brought spices. These friends of Jesus wrapped His lifeless frame with graveclothes soaked in costly balms and reverently placed His corpse in the sepulcher. They rolled the stone against the door of that rock-hewn tomb, Pilate sealed it, and soldiers stood guard.

The disciples gathered in the upper room, but already some of the band were planning to leave town. Their hopes had been buried in Joseph's tomb. The Redeemer was dead. The King had been crucified instead of crowned. Nothing remained but dreams of what might have been—if there had been no Herod, no Caiaphas, no Annas, no Pilate, no mob.

Let us imagine we are interviewing Peter, James, and John. "Say there, brothers. What's the problem?"

"Jesus is dead. It's all over."

"What are you going to do?"

"We're going to hide out for a few days until the authorities relax their vigil. Then we're going back to Galilee. Peter thinks he might return to fishing."

"Thomas, what's your opinion?"

"Mine? I had my doubts all along. Now they are confirmed. I loved Jesus, but now He's dead, and that's all there is to it."

"How about you, Nathanael? Do you still think that no good thing can come out of Nazareth?"

"Oh, Jesus was good, all right. That's the trouble. He was too good for this wicked world. He should have stayed in Nazareth. He should never have come to Jerusalem. Jerusalem always stones the prophets and kills those God sends to it. He said so Himself. Now it has killed Him. It's all over."

What a pity Job wasn't one of the apostles! Do you know what Job would have said? He would have said, "I know that my redeemer liveth. Just wait a few days. He will rise from the dead."

Job believed in the resurrection of Christ, and he was right! The past two millennia have vindicated him. "The Lord is risen indeed" (Luke 24:34). Job's Redeemer lives!

## III. THE RETURN OF CHRIST

Job's faith soared and, seeing what few (if any) of the Old Testament prophets saw, said, "I know that my redeemer

liveth, and that he shall stand at the latter day upon the earth."
He saw and understood both comings of Christ: His coming to
redeem and His coming to rule. Christ's first coming would
climax in a resurrection; His second coming "at the latter day"
would climax in a reign.

Many Old Testament passages reveal that when the
Redeemer stands on the earth "at the latter day," the geography
and ecology of this planet will change remarkably. The Lord's
pierced feet will alight on the mount of Olives, which will
instantly split in two. A river will flow from Jerusalem (Ezekiel
47:1-12), and the Dead Sea will be cleansed of its salts. The
effects of the curse (Genesis 3:17-19) will be put under restraint
so that abundant harvests will be reaped throughout the whole
world. Deserts will blossom as the rose and the earth will
become a global garden of Eden.

Governmental changes will also occur. The world's
superpowers will have been swept away during the dreadful
judgments of the great tribulation and the battle of Armaged-
don. The scattered remnants of the Gentile peoples will be
summoned to the valley of Jehoshaphat for judgment. Only a
small number of Jews and Gentiles will enter the millennial
kingdom. Every one of these will be saved, sanctified, and
Spirit-filled.

Jesus will reign over the world with a rod of iron.
Jerusalem will be His capital, the new temple will be the center
of all worship, and everyone will have knowledge of God. The
Jewish people will administer the everyday affairs of Christ's
empire, and all immorality, injustice, and wickedness will be
suppressed.

The earth will become the center of interest for the entire
universe, and the old hymn will prove itself true at last:

> Jesus shall reign, where'er the sun
> Doth his successive journeys run;
> His kingdom stretch from shore to shore,
> Till moons shall wax and wane no more.[2]

Job lived long before the prophets penned their glowing pages, but he saw the whole prophetic picture. He may not have seen it in detail—what is still sketchy to us must have been even more vague and hazy to him. Yet what he saw gave him hope. Sitting in dust and ashes, covered with boils, mourning his dead, cursed by his wife, and goaded by his friends, he had the assurance that Jesus would "stand at the latter day upon the earth."

## IV. THE RELATIONSHIP OF CHRIST

The godly man who could speak so confidently of the redemption of Christ, the resurrection of Christ, and the return of Christ, had the vision to see that he had a personal stake in these facts. This insight translated truth for Job out of the realm of the theoretical and theological into the realm of the personal and practical.

The same law of God that would raise Christ from the dead would raise him! Anticipating Paul's words about the resurrection by hundreds upon hundreds of years, Job said, "Though after my skin worms destroy this body, yet in my flesh shall I see God: Whom I shall see for myself, and mine eyes shall behold, and not another" (Job 19:26-27). Job was speaking of things that in his day were thousands of years in the future. Christ would come to redeem the world more than fifteen hundred years after Job spoke and we are still waiting for Him to return.

Confident of his stake in the resurrection, Job was saying in effect, "Death is not the end. Beyond death is resurrection. The resurrection of my Redeemer will be the unconditional guarantee of my resurrection as well. Though worms destroy my body, *in my flesh* shall I see God!" Job believed that although his body would be reduced to the dust from which it came, he would in that same body see his Redeemer at some future date.

We can imagine Job applying his faith in various situations

and saying, "I don't know how it works, but I know that it does."

First we see him looking into the dark depths of a tomb. He sees the horror of a corpse rotting away and becoming a mere bundle of bones with a grinning skull and then nothing but dust. He says, "I know there is an organic union between the Redeemer and the redeemed, a union so vital and so real that His resurrection is both the proof and the guarantee of ours. I don't know how it works, but I know that it does."

Next we see Job standing on a hill and looking intently at the setting sun. As it dips below the rim of the world, the evening shadows gather quickly. They lengthen and swallow up the day. Night falls and Job says, "I know I haven't seen the last of that sun. Tomorrow it will rise. It will come up beyond the hills behind me and climb once more to the sky above me. I don't know how it works, but I know that it does."

Then we see Job standing beside a tree. Its summer foliage has turned to a blaze of yellows, reds, and browns. Its sap has begun to sink and soon winter winds will strip away the dead leaves. The tree will stand bleak and bare, waving its naked branches before the icy blasts. Job says, "I have seen all this before. Four or five moons from now that tree will blossom again. I don't know how it works, but I know that it does."

Again we see Job, this time looking at some dry seeds in his hand. He digs a little furrow in the ground, drops the seeds in, and covers them with soil. He says, "Those seeds will rot away, but before long I will see new life springing from the ground where I planted them. I don't know how it works, but I know that it does."

We also see Job watching a bear preparing for the winter months. He says, "That bear will soon vanish into some dark hole in which he will curl up and hibernate. Months will come and go while he sleeps a sleep that is almost akin to death. Then spring will call and the bear will wake up. I don't know how it works, but I know that it does."

We can almost read Job's mind as he reflects on all the

scenes he has observed: *I don't understand how these things work, but I know that they do. The sun rises and sets according to the law of the stars. Dead seeds bring forth new life according to the law of the soil, and the earth is carpeted with green. Trees shed their leaves and stand like sad sentinels through the weary watches of winter and, according to the law of the seasons, bud again in the spring. Bears hibernate until, according to the law of the species, they are stirred to new life after their long winter's nap. My beloved children are buried in the cemetery behind my house. Soon I will join them in the grave. But according to the law of the soul, we will rise again. I don't know how it works, but I know that it does. Although worms will destroy my body, in my body I will see God.*

Job—like a pioneer of the faith, like a prospector in the old West who has struck gold—staked his claim in the resurrection of Christ. We too can stake our claim. If we take the quantum leap of faith and exclaim, "My Redeemer!" then we can also say, "Though worms destroy this body, yet in my flesh shall I see God."

---

1. From "Blessed Assurance" by Fanny J. Crosby.
2. From "Jesus Shall Reign" by Isaac Watts.

# 6
# Jochebed
# and Her Boy

*Hebrews 11:23-26*

---

I. SHE HAD HIM
II. SHE HID HIM
III. SHE HELD HIM

---

Moses towers like a titan across the vast reaches of our Bible. He is mentioned in 261 verses in Exodus, 80 verses in Leviticus, 216 verses in Numbers, 35 verses in Deuteronomy, 51 verses in Joshua, and 47 verses in the other historical books. The book of Psalms and the prophets also refer to him. He is mentioned in 37 verses in the Gospels, 19 verses in Acts, and 22 verses in the Epistles. The book of Revelation also refers to him. Altogether he is mentioned in 784 verses in the Bible: 705 in the Old Testament and 79 in the New Testament. Pity the people whose pastors don't believe in Moses. By the time such liberals try to tear him out of the Scriptures, they don't have much of a Bible left.

Moses is one of the greatest men God ever made. Known as the emancipator and lawgiver of Israel, he was also a scholar, soldier, statesman, and saint. He was one of the two men who were sent back from the other world to confer with

Christ on the mount of transfiguration (Matthew 17:1-8). He wrote the first song of Scripture (Exodus 15:1-19) and in glory they still sing "the song of Moses...and the song of the Lamb" (Revelation 15:3). Much of the credit for what he became must be given to his mother Jochebed.

# I. SHE HAD HIM

Before Moses was born, the pharaoh had decreed that every male child born to a Hebrew woman was to be thrown into the Nile. This decree, one of Satan's early efforts to prevent the birth of the Messiah by attacking the Jewish race, must have been a tremendous test of Amram and Jochebed's faith. Their little boy, who was destined to rule the Israelites, was born, like Christ, with a great red dragon waiting to devour him. The couple had two older children, but the Bible does not record their births. Perhaps they were born before the edict.

Few women have had to raise a family in more difficult circumstances. The fact that a Moses, a Miriam, and an Aaron could come from a slave hut on the Nile says a lot about Jochebed's influence.

Hebrews 11:23 links the faith of Moses to the faith of his mother and father: "By faith Moses, when he was born, was hid three months of his parents, because they saw he was a proper child; and they were not afraid of the king's commandment." The king's wrath was something to be reckoned with, but they discounted it because they feared the wrath of God far more. They made up their minds not to murder their child in cold blood just to comply with the tyrannical edict of a wicked king. God, in turn, honored their faith.

Many parents would have decided not to have any more children under the circumstances. But Moses was born and the dragon of the Nile roared in vain.

The hour had struck for the Hebrews to be emancipated from Egypt. The prophecy given to Abraham about four centuries earlier (Genesis 15:13-14) was about to be fulfilled.

The nation that Satan wanted to stamp out of existence was about to rise up and trample the world. To accomplish His purpose, God sent a baby into the world.

That is usually God's way, as F. W. Boreham observed as he looked at the year 1809. That year stood midway between two great battles that shaped the destiny of the world: the battle of Trafalgar, which destroyed the naval might of Napoleon; and the battle of Waterloo, which destroyed his military might. Everyone was thinking of battles. Nobody was thinking of babies; yet in that one year William Gladstone was born in Liverpool, Lord Alfred Tennyson was born in Somersby, Oliver Wendell Holmes was born in Massachusetts, Abraham Lincoln was born in Kentucky, Frederick Chopin was born in Warsaw, and Felix Mendelsohn was born in Hamburg. Boreham commented:

> Viewing that age in the truer perspective which the years enable us to command, we may well ask ourselves which of the battles of 1809 mattered more than the babies of 1809. When a wrong wants righting or a work wants doing, or a truth wants preaching, or a continent wants opening, God sends a baby into the world to do it. That is why, long, long ago, a Babe was born at Bethlehem.[1]

And that is why, long before the birth of Jesus, another babe was born in a slave hut on the banks of the Nile.

Jochebed believed that God is greater than pharaoh, that Satan is no match for the Holy Spirit, and that "greater is he that is in you, than he that is in the world" (1 John 4:4). So she had Moses and we can thank God that she did. Mosaic law lies at the heart of every sane piece of legislation on the world's statute books. The books of Moses form the Torah or Pentateuch—the first five majestic, monumental books of the Bible. Without them we would be immeasurably impoverished in our understanding of God's ways. By giving us the Pentateuch,

Moses laid the foundation for all the subsequent books of the Bible—and a massive foundation it is.

## II. SHE HID HIM

As long as they could, Jochebed and Amram shielded baby Moses from the destructive powers of the world by hiding him within the four walls of their humble home. Nothing in that home could harm a little child. Thank God for homes like theirs!

Some of us were raised in homes like that of Jochebed and Amram. We never saw an alcoholic beverage or a pack of cigarettes in the house and we were not allowed to watch television except when strictly supervised. Are we bringing up our families in homes like those of our mothers and fathers? What a terrible thing it would be if one of our children turned to drink and, putting the blame on his parents' consciences, said to them, "Well, you drank. You kept a bottle in the refrigerator."

The great red dragon hates our children and wants to destroy them. As long as possible, we should shelter and shield them from the world's destructive influences. Think of the violence, immorality, and perversion in many of today's television shows; the vileness of outright pornography on cable television; the foul lyrics and soul-destroying ideas in most popular contemporary music. Are we hiding our children from these influences?

Our homes should be places where goodness and godliness are constantly taught and exemplified even during a child's earliest days. His soul's citadel must be stormed then, for it will be ten thousand times harder to capture later on.

Jochebed kept baby Moses home as long as possible, but the time came when the infant could no longer be hidden there. That time comes—at a later age of course—for today's children too. They have to go to school, where they are exposed to other children whose parents may smoke, drink, watch violent or sexually explicit movies, curse, gamble, and engage in immorality. Our children have to sit in classrooms where they may be exposed to humanistic teachers who hate God, reject Moses in favor of Darwin, and advocate perverted values. Our children may have to rub shoulders with fellow students who take drugs, drink, and engage in premarital sex. Then what do we do?

When baby Moses could no longer be hidden at home, Amram probably said to Jochebed, "What do we do now?"

Jochebed may have answered by asking another question: "How does God save someone who is condemned to death?"

Then they would have thought of the ark. When God condemned the wicked antediluvian world to death, He told Noah to build an ark in order to save his family from being destroyed by the flood. That ark was to be covered inside and out with pitch. When it was finished, Noah and his family went into the ark and the storms of judgment came. The rain beat upon the ark, but the people inside were saved. We can almost hear Amram and Jochebed saying, "That is how God saves people who are condemned to death."

Knowing that God is the same yesterday, today, and forever, they decided to make a little ark and cover it with pitch, just as Noah did. They put their baby in the ark and placed it in the waters of the Nile, where destructive forces lurked. Amram and Jochebed committed Moses to the ark, which would come between him and those destructive forces. "We cannot save our little boy from the forces of death," Moses' parents surely said, "but God can." God always honors faith like theirs.

In Scripture the ark always represents Christ. Today we must commit our little ones to Him, just as Jochebed and Amram committed Moses to the ark. We cannot save our children, but He can. "The promise is unto you, and to your children," said Peter (Acts 2:39). By a deliberate act of believing faith that is backed by the power of godly lives, Christian parents must commit their children to Christ. He alone can surround them with an adequate protective influence once they have to venture out beyond the confines of their homes.

## III. SHE HELD HIM

Of all the "coincidences" that have changed the fortunes of this weary world, among the greatest are the events surrounding the discovery of the baby Moses in his ark. We know the story well. The royal princess (believed by many to be Hatshepsut, one of the most forceful, imperial, and powerful of all those who rose to power in Egypt) found that little ark of bulrushes. She sent her maid to fetch it, and just when it was opened, the baby wept!

No woman's heart could have resisted the whimper of that lovely little boy. Perhaps he was hungry. Perhaps he was wet. Perhaps the sudden light startled him. Perhaps he was afraid of the strange hands that held him up for the princess to see. In any case, the tears that trickled down the cheek of that baby melted the heart of pharaoh's proud daughter, and changed the destiny of an empire and the fate of the world. "This is a Hebrew boy," she said in effect. "He's supposed to be thrown into the Nile. I'll adopt him. I'll take him home and raise him as my son."

Jochebed had not left her baby alone in his ark. His sister Miriam watched over him. Likewise when we commit our children to Christ, God still expects us to take all the prudent measures we can to shield them. He does not bless carelessness and lack of common sense.

As soon as Miriam saw what was happening, she came closer to the water. With commendable presence of mind she spoke to the princess. "My lady," she said in effect, "do you need a nurse for that child?"

The princess had not thought of that. Of course she needed a nurse. The baby was not yet weaned. We can imagine her commanding Miriam: "Fetch a Hebrew slave to nurse this child for me. Tell the woman that I will pay her." So Jochebed received wages for raising her own son! God always rewards His children for doing those things that please Him—if not in this life, in the world to come.

We do not know how long the princess allowed Jochebed to nurse Moses. Often in those days a child was not weaned for several years. (Isaac seems to have been five years of age when he was weaned.) No doubt this godly woman took full advantage of the few years she had. Before he went out into the world, she wanted to drill truth into his plastic mind in a way that he would never forget. What did she teach him? It does not take much thought to answer that question. We just have to look at the book of Genesis.

Moses later wrote four books of the Bible out of his own experience: Exodus, Leviticus, Numbers, and Deuteronomy. But in Genesis he recorded the truths his mother had passed down to him—truths that were modified, amplified, and confirmed to him by the inspiration of the Spirit of God.

Surely Jochebed said to herself, *I don't have long but, God helping me, I'm going to get the word of God into this child before the professors of Egypt try to fill his mind with foolish philosophies.* She taught him the truth about creation, Cain and Abel, Enoch, Noah and the flood, the tower of Babel, Abraham and the covenant, Sodom and Gomorrah, Lot and his wife, Ishmael and Isaac, Jacob and Esau, and the twelve patriarchs. Jochebed told Moses why the Hebrew people were slaves in Egypt and taught him about the prophecy that after four hundred years they would be delivered.

Above all she taught him about Joseph, a young man who lived for God in the same royal courts to which Moses would soon be taken. She told him how Joseph was sold as a slave in Egypt; how in spite of his very impressionable age, he took his stand against the impurity and immorality of Potiphar's wife; how he suffered for his godliness; and how God raised him up at last to a place at the right hand of pharaoh. Jochebed's emphasis here is reflected in the fact that Moses devoted one-fourth of the book of Genesis to the story of Joseph.

The Jesuits used to say, "Give us a child until he's seven, and you can do what you like with him after that." We know that Jochebed would have agreed with them because she did a thorough job of training Moses.

Eventually the order came from the palace: "Send me Moses." As Jochebed kissed Moses goodbye, she probably said, "Remember what I've taught you, my son." Moses never forgot that he was a Hebrew. The universities of Egypt, the temptations of the palace, the lure of position, power, wealth, and a worldly throne never erased his mother's training.

Jochebed, a daughter of Levi who married another descendant of Levi, doubtless devoted herself to the Levitical duties of prayer after Moses left home. This was centuries before an office of prayer was founded in Israel. What a woman! What an example! What a challenge to us!

---

1.  F. W. Boreham, My Christmas Book (Grand Rapids: Zondervan, 1953) 7.

# 7
# Aaron
# and His Call

*Exodus 4:14-18,27-31*

I. AARON RECOGNIZED BY GOD

II. AARON REDIRECTED BY GOD

   A. To Be a Preacher

   B. To Be a Priest

      1. Aaron's Symbolic Consecration

         a. His Ablution

         b. His Apparel

         c. His Acceptance

      2. Aaron's Sublime Calling

III. AARON RESTRICTED BY GOD

IV. AARON REPLACED BY GOD

   A. His Priestly Failure

   B. His Parental Failure

   C. His Personal Failure

Aaron's younger brother Moses grew up to become one of the greatest people in history. Aaron's sister Miriam was courageous and clever. Occasionally she prophesied and she had a strong dose of common sense. So Aaron came from a gifted family. And he was gifted. He rose to the highest position a man could occupy among God's people in those days. He became Israel's first high priest, from whom all other Hebrew priests would descend until the coming of Christ.

Aaron, Miriam, and Moses were born in a slave hut in the Jewish ghetto in the land of Goshen on the Nile. When Aaron was a boy, the ruling pharaoh established a program to wipe out the Jews—slowly, surely, and systematically (Exodus 1:15-22). The imperial edict did not apply to Aaron, but the sword of slavery, oppression, and genocide pierced Aaron's soul. Moses escaped death because he was adopted as a baby by the Egyptian royal family. He moved to the palace at a young age, so Aaron did not know Moses well. The worlds in which the brothers lived were poles apart.

## I. AARON RECOGNIZED BY GOD

"I know that [Aaron] can speak well," God said to Moses (Exodus 4:14). What a gift of oratory Aaron must have had! Word of his eloquence had reached up to Heaven itself. His golden tongue was a topic of conversation even around the throne of God. We can imagine God confiding to Michael or Gabriel, "That man Aaron is a very good speaker. One of these days I will be able to use a man who has such a winsome way with words."

Aaron was gifted, but not great. He did not excel as a scholar, thinker, or leader, but he knew a man who did: his younger brother Moses. Although the two brothers were not intimately acquainted, Aaron no doubt had seen or heard about Moses from time to time. Moses had the reputation of being one of the greatest scholars ever to graduate from the universities of Egypt. The Bible says he was "learned in all the wisdom of the Egyptians" (Acts 7:22). He was a trained diplomat, soldier, and statesman and a born leader.

But Moses was banished from the court and the country

for siding with the Hebrews against the antisemitic throne. He was in exile, somewhere in Sinai. *What a pity,* Aaron probably thought, *that Moses made such a mess of things! If ever there was a man who could have delivered Israel out of bondage, it was Moses. If ever there was a man made for such a mission and trained for such a mission, it was Moses. If ever there was a man with a heart big enough and bold enough, that man was Moses.*

We can picture Aaron one day being overcome by an urge from God to look for his long-lost brother and setting out for Horeb. He would use his eloquence to persuade Moses to become the kinsman-redeemer of the downtrodden people of God.

We can almost hear God saying, "There goes Aaron. I can use him now. First I'll prepare Moses for his arrival. I'll tell Moses to go back to Egypt with Aaron to emancipate his people. I'll say to Moses, "[Aaron] shall be thy spokesman unto the people: and he shall be, even he shall be to thee instead of a mouth, and thou shalt be to him instead of God" (Exodus 4:16). Aaron would be the prophet of Moses. God would speak to Moses, who would speak to Aaron, who would speak to the people and to pharaoh.

God recognized Aaron's speaking ability because He made him. Likewise He knows our gifts, talents, and abilities. He has a plan and purpose for each of our lives, just as He had a plan and purpose for Aaron. Surely there could not be a worse tragedy than to miss God's plan. What a pity it would be to fritter away our gifts without ever finding out why God gave them to us or how He wants them used!

## II. AARON REDIRECTED BY GOD

### A. To Be a Preacher

Little did Aaron know when he picked up his staff, sneaked out of that ghetto, and left Goshen to find Moses, that he would come back to Egypt as a prophet. But that is what happened.

Whereas Moses knew what he wanted to say but might stumble over his words, Aaron always had the right words and could communicate ideas with clarity and convicting power. When Moses was a young man, he was "mighty in words" (Acts 7:22), but the long hours he spent alone in the desert must have blunted that ability. Besides, he probably had not spoken Hebrew or Egyptian for many years. Thus Aaron's gift of oratory must have been a great help to Moses in persuading the Israelites that the crisis hour had come when God would liberate His people.

We can imagine that even Aaron was at first a little shy about speaking to pharaoh. Perhaps Aaron said to Moses, "It's one thing to minister encouragement to God's people—to exhort, rebuke, comfort, and reassure. I know I can do that. But I'm afraid I'd be absolutely tongue-tied in the presence of the pharaoh's awesome majesty. I don't have enough education. I'd be far too nervous to speak out in the lavish surroundings of the royal palace."

"Nonsense!" Moses would have replied. "Pharaoh's just a poor lost sinner like anyone else. Besides, I'll tell you what to say."

There is a lesson in this for the person who is called to minister to a group of people but feels inadequate for the task. He may not be a great thinker and may not have had the opportunity to obtain much schooling. Such a person should find a Moses—someone who has greater gifts than he has—and ask the gifted individual to expound the Word of God to him. A person who has little originality or learning of his own should read books written by those who do have insight. Then he can share what he has learned with others.

Reader, if you feel inadequate, you should go searching for a Moses—even if you have to sell your home and live on one meal a day to pay your way to Horeb. Do not rest until you find teachers who minister to your soul.

Aaron became a very successful preacher. On the night of the first Passover, he saw the fruit of his preaching. Millions of people entered into the truth of redemption through the shed blood of a lamb. Surely that thrilled his soul. After the Hebrews had sheltered themselves beneath the blood and set out for Canaan, perhaps God said to Gabriel, "I told you Aaron could speak well!"

Then God redirected Aaron. Instead of continuing to use him as a preacher, God reshaped his ministry. That great mass of converts no longer needed an evangelist; they needed a pastor. So God guided Aaron into the priesthood.

## B. To Be a Priest

Aaron was the first in a long line of men who were the leaders of the only true religion in the world, a religion that retained its power and authority until the crucifixion of Christ. Aaron and his descendants were the only men who ever had sanction from God to function as mediators between God and man in a ritualistic, religious system. God called Aaron to the priesthood because, as Hebrews 5:4 says, "No man taketh this honour unto himself."

### 1. Aaron's Symbolic Consecration

Aaron's ablution, apparel, and acceptance marked his ordination to the priestly ministry in Israel (Exodus 28–29; Leviticus 8–9). First there was his *ablution*. Before anything else could take place, he had to be cleansed. God does not insist that His ministers be clever, but He does insist that they be clean. Aaron was only a feeble, faltering man; his subsequent sin in making the golden calf showed how frail he was. So Aaron needed to be cleansed.

Then there was the putting on of his *apparel*. Aaron needed to be suitably clothed for the functions he had to perform. Since his priesthood was essentially ritualistic, his apparel had symbolic significance. Each garment spoke of the perfection of Christ, our Great High Priest.

Aaron's coat of fine twined linen symbolized the perfect humanity of the Lord Jesus. The beautiful embroidery on that coat symbolized the inherent beauty of the Lord's character.

The blue of Aaron's robe reminds us that the Lord Jesus was the One from Heaven. The fact that his robe was seamless and could not be torn reminds us that all of Satan's efforts to rend the deity of Christ or find a hole in His perfection were doomed to fail. Jesus could not sin.

Bells and pomegranates were fastened to the skirt of Aaron's robe. The pomegranates symbolized fruitfulness. The tinkling bells drew attention to the walk of the priest as he went about his duties as mediator between God and man. The fact that the bells and pomegranates were equal in number reminds us of the perfect balance that the Lord Jesus always exhibited as He walked through this world. He was perfectly faithful and always fruitful.

The gorgeous ephod, which was slipped over Aaron's head and fastened under his arms, held the breastplate in place. The breastplate was a piece of cloth studded with twelve precious stones—one for each of the twelve tribes of Israel. The names of the tribes were engraved on these stones, so whenever the high priest went about his official duties in the holy place of the tabernacle, he carried the names of the tribes over his heart. Thus the breastplate reminds us of our glorious Lord, who loves us with an everlasting love and knows us all by name. He carries our names on His heart and remembers us in the holy place on high.

Aaron's miter was a white linen turban to which was attached a plate of pure gold. Engraved on this plate were the words "HOLINESS TO THE LORD." The miter reminds us of both the headship and the holiness of Christ. His absolute supremacy over God's people can never be challenged or changed.

Every garment that Aaron put on was intended to remind him that he represented Another. The Jewish priest was the representative on earth of the Lord Jesus Christ in Heaven. Today every minister, missionary, and Sunday school teacher must represent the Lord Jesus. Otherwise their ministries cannot be effective. All that they do and say should draw attention to Christ. Now, all of us believers are priests, so we must all be clothed in the righteousness of Christ and display His glory and grace.

Finally we note Aaron's *acceptance* into the priesthood. After being cleansed and clothed, he ministered at the brazen altar and the golden altar. He stood in the holy place, bathed in the light of the lampstand, and contemplated the bread on the table. Once a year he was permitted to enter the holy of holies itself and minister in the immediate presence of God. Once a year he passed beyond the veil and stood before the sacred ark, the mercy seat, and the cherubim in the full blaze of that awesome shekinah glory in which God dwelt, and God accepted him.

## 2. Aaron's Sublime Calling

Aaron's calling was to meet the needs of God's people. He assisted the poor and ministered at the brazen altar in the outer court of the tabernacle. There he instructed the people about the five major offerings (the sin offering, the trespass offering, the meal offering, the peace offering, and the burnt offering), assisted them in getting right with God, and lead them on to communion and true worship. When people came to him with their burdens of sin, he in effect pointed them to Calvary, for all the offerings focused on truth concerning Christ and the cross.

Aaron also ministered at the golden altar. There he burned incense and filled the holy place with fragrance. Clouds of perfumed smoke ascended, depicting the ministry of prayer and intercession.

Aaron ministered in the holy place as well. He made sure that the golden lampstand was always burning brightly and one day a week he enjoyed all the food that was on the table. With his fellow priests he feasted symbolically on Christ, the Bread of Heaven.

Such was the sublime calling to which God redirected

Aaron. No vocation on earth was higher than his—not even a king's. A king was called to wield secular power, but the high priest was called to wield spiritual power.

## III. AARON RESTRICTED BY GOD

The priesthood in Israel failed almost as soon as it began. Aaron's sons Nadab and Abihu offered "strange fire" before the Lord (Leviticus 10:1). Instead of using the fire that had come down from Heaven, they kindled their own fire and God summarily judged them. Fire flashed out from Him and consumed them both.

God still does not want "strange fire"—that is, work done in the energy of the flesh instead of in the power of the Holy Spirit. A great deal of "strange fire" is all too evident in Christian ministries today.

Because of the abuse of spiritual power by Aaron's sons, God instructed Moses to restrict Aaron's access to His divine presence (Leviticus 16:1-2). Instead of entering the holy of holies whenever he pleased, Aaron was allowed to go in only on the day of atonement. Even then, the most elaborate ritualistic preparation had to precede his approach. No less than forty-six separate steps had to be taken before Aaron would be permitted to enter the presence of God. Each step had a symbolic meaning pointing directly to the work of Christ at Calvary.

Thank God those restrictions are now removed and the intricate rituals concerning the day of atonement have been abolished! Calvary blazed a trail for us right into the heavenly holy of holies. We can come by that "new and living way...through the veil, that is to say, his flesh" (Hebrews 10:20). Our Great High Priest enthroned on high has fulfilled all that was symbolized by the ritual of the two goats. One was slain to picture Jesus as the One who would shed His blood. The other was laden with the people's sins and taken away to "a land not inhabited" (Leviticus 16:22), thus picturing Jesus as the One who would bear our sin. In this ritual we see Jesus carrying our sins outside the camp so that we could come inside the veil. Hallelujah!

The restrictions God placed on the priesthood remind us how our disobedience to the Word of God limits our usefulness. God will not tolerate self-will in His service. If we persist in asserting our own will, He will restrict us too.

# IV. AARON REPLACED BY GOD

Because Aaron was only a man, he died and had to be replaced by another high priest. In time that high priest also died and had to be replaced. And so it went on for fifteen hundred years. Human failure, frailty, and mortality necessitated constant change until the priesthood of Christ replaced the Aaronic priesthood.

By the time of Christ the sacred office had become a political prize held by Annas and Caiaphas, a pair of scoundrels indeed. Aaron himself had failed as a priest, as a parent, and as a person.

## A. His Priestly Failure

With Moses nearby to guide, strengthen, and support him, Aaron could function well. He could scatter the objections of the children of Israel and even beard the lion Pharaoh in his den. But while Moses was up on the holy mount for forty days and forty nights, Aaron was like a reed shaking in the wind. The absence of Moses revealed the littleness of Aaron.

The people in the valley below became increasingly restless and hard to handle. They said to Aaron, "Up, make us gods, which shall go before us; for as for this Moses...we wot not what is become of him" (Exodus 32:1). Giving in to the crowd's riotous clamor, Aaron took their golden ornaments and made a molten calf similar to the idols they had seen in Egypt.

A man may be able to speak well when everyone is

applauding him or when certain key people are lending their solid support. Yet the same man may prove to be weak and helpless when stormy weather comes and he is left alone in a leadership position. Aaron was such a person. He had no backbone, no courage, and no conviction. He had grown so used to speaking for Moses that he had lost all power to speak for himself. Aaron should have been willing to say no to the mob even if they threatened to tear him to pieces. Instead he placated them by agreeing to make that golden calf and permitting them to engage in lustful, idolatrous behavior. He wanted the approval of the multitude.

Aaron's love for applause led him into terrible sin. His failure was tragic, but in the end it doubtless made him a priest who understood other people's infirmities.

## B. His Parental Failure

Aaron was unable to make two of his sons—Nadab and Abihu—understand the seriousness of handling holy things. He could not stop them from offering "strange fire" and probably did not even know they intended to do so. Aaron paid a high price for this lack of parental control: as noted before, he saw his sons devoured by God's flaming wrath. Moreover Moses forbade him to show his grief, since Nadab and Abihu deserved to die. Aaron needed to uphold the holiness of God before the people even when that holiness brought judgment on those he loved best.

Those who are called and consecrated to a pastoral ministry can be certain that if they do not discipline their children, God will—especially if the misbehavior of the children dishonors Him.

## C. His Personal Failure

Aaron seems to have been too easily influenced by his sister Miriam. For example, he was swayed by her to criticize Moses because of his marriage to an Ethiopian woman. It was no business of theirs whom Moses married. That matter was between Moses and God. But Miriam, motivated by racial prejudice, lashed out against Moses. And Aaron, carried away by Miriam, joined in the gossip and harsh words. Their attack on Moses showed how small-minded they were and threatened his authority. Judgment followed swiftly, for we read in Numbers 12:10 that God smote Miriam with leprosy. Aaron escaped punishment solely on account of God's respect for the high office he held.

When Aaron was 123 years old, he died. Numbers 20:22-29 draws a sad picture of Aaron being stripped of his priestly robes and being laid to rest in a wilderness grave on the wrong side of Jordan. But let us take our eyes off Aaron and fix them on Christ, who never fails. The Holy Spirit says of Him:

> Thou art a priest for ever after the order of Melchisedec. Who in the days of his flesh, when he had offered up prayers and supplications with strong crying and tears unto him that was able to save him from death, and was heard in that he feared; Though he were a Son, yet learned he obedience by the things which he suffered; And being made perfect, he became the author of eternal salvation unto all them that obey him; Called of God an high priest after the order of Melchisedec (Hebrews 5:6-10).

In the end Aaron, like all of God's workers, was replaced. God buries His workers, but the work of God goes on.

# 8
# Balaam
# and His Curse

*2 Peter 2:15-16*

> I. A VERY GREAT PROBLEM
> II. A VERY GOOD PREACHER
>> A. His Prophetic Preaching
>> B. His Practical Preaching
>>> 1. Transparent Honesty
>>> 2. Tender Humanity
>>> 3. True Humility
> III. A VERY GRAVE PERIL

Balaam is the epitome of an apostate. He knew the truth and was able to preach the truth, but he sold it for temporal advantage and worldly gain.

## I. A VERY GREAT PROBLEM

When we read about Balaam we are confronted with some problems. The first is the superficial problem of Balaam's donkey. It actually spoke to him and remonstrated with him for being so merciless and reckless with his whip (Numbers 22:21-33).

Somebody once said to D. L. Moody, "Surely, Mr. Moody, you don't believe that story in the Bible where it says that the donkey spoke to Balaam?"

"Oh yes," replied Mr. Moody, "I believe that. There's really nothing very difficult about it at all. You make a donkey and I'll make it speak."

It was no harder for God to enable Balaam's donkey to speak than it was for God to enable Balaam to speak.

The deeper problem that confronts us is why God used Balaam. Balaam was a soothsayer. Today we would call him a psychic, a spiritist, a medium, or a person with a "familiar spirit." Yet God used him to deliver some of the most astonishing messages recorded in the Bible—prophecies that are coming into fresh focus today.

Balaam was a Gentile, an alien to the commonwealth of Israel, and a stranger to the covenants of grace. He had no part or interest in those exceedingly great and precious promises that were all "yea and amen" to the people of God. The promises made to Abraham, Isaac, and Jacob were all signed and sealed, but they were not for Balaam. He was a pagan priest, a hireling prophet, an avaricious trafficker in potions and spells.

We are very much in the dark as to how and when Balaam obtained the knowledge of the truth of God that he seems to have possessed. He came from the same part of the world as Abraham, and that might furnish a clue. When Abraham left Ur of the Chaldees hundreds of years earlier, he left behind him a remarkable testimony. Perhaps some echoes of his response to God's call lingered among the people of his native land.

God can speak to whomever He chooses, whenever He desires, by any means He prefers. Usually He speaks through the Bible, but we must not try to limit God. When a man does not have a Bible and does not even know that the Bible exists, God communicates with him in other ways. God imparted truth to men such as Melchizedek, Job, and Jethro, none of whom had a Bible. As Dan Crawford, pioneer missionary to Africa, once said, "God can certainly speak to those to whom He does not write." So somehow, somewhere, God spoke to Balaam, and Balaam knew that God had spoken to him. Moreover, King Balak of Moab knew that God had spoken to Balaam. "The true Light, which lighteth every man that cometh into the world" (John 1:9) must have blazed with special brilliance in the soul of Balaam.

Balaam preached from the lofty heights of Pisgah just a few years before Moses looked down from the same mountain peak over the length and breadth of the promised land, then fell asleep in the arms of God. Balaam's sermons contain some of the most penetrating eschatology in the Bible, particularly in relation to the future of the nation of Israel. They carry added weight because they are the testimony of a hostile witness.

Balaam had no love for Israel and would have been just as happy to curse her as to prophesy her future. But prophesy he did. Not even Moses, Micah, or Malachi foretold greater events than this hireling prophet from the Euphrates predicted.

Then too, Balaam's sermons on the subject of salvation are doctrinally sound. They are masterpieces of soteriology, unsurpassed until the apostle Paul wrote the Epistle to the Romans. Moreover Balaam presented these truths with astonishing courage, disregarding the consequences. Court preachers are not usually inclined to lay unpalatable truths before the one who sits on the throne!

Nevertheless Balaam has been in a lost eternity for more than three thousand years. He has been suffering the vengeance of eternal fire, and the flames have no doubt been made hotter for him because he once knew the truth of God. He preached to others, yet he himself became a castaway. He suffers the pangs of unavailing remorse that are the portion of those who once clearly saw what salvation was all about, but had no use for it and taught others to tread wrong paths.

Centuries after Balaam died, the Lord Jesus warned, "If

therefore the light that is in thee be darkness, how great is that darkness!" (Matthew 6:23) This principle still applies. We cannot turn away from the truth and not embrace a lie. There is no delusion so dark as that which possesses the soul of a person who has known the truth and has forsaken it.

Balaam mistook divine light for divine life; he preached the truth but did not practice it; his behavior did not square with his profession. Indeed Balaam's story is a beacon exposing the special peril of the preacher who substitutes a public exposition of truth for a personal experience of truth.

Balaam had two consuming lusts that damned him in the end. He had a lust for women and a lust for wealth. He had a dirty mind and he loved money. He would do anything for money. Balaam would alter his message to please his audience if it meant a bigger honorarium. Worse still, he was a sly, lewd, and greedy man when he was out of the pulpit.

God knew all about Balaam and used him just the same. But having used him, He abandoned him to his pornography and his purse.

## II. A VERY GOOD PREACHER

In spite of the fact that Balaam was an apostate and a rogue, he knew how to preach. He could have filled the biggest pulpit in our country today. An orator who had learned how to drive home his points, he knew that he could throw dust in a man's eyes for a long time, provided he did it eloquently.

We can picture Balaam sitting in his suburban home near the Euphrates and his servant running in to announce that an important-looking caravan is approaching. Balaam goes out to see who is coming and finds at his doorstep an impressive delegation from the imperial court of Balak, king of Moab. They have come specifically to invite Balaam to preach for the king. (Balaam always knew he was good, but he hadn't realized he was this good! There was no engagement in

Mesopotamia that he would not cancel in order to accept an invitation like this!) The ambassador presents him with a letter:

Dear Dr. Balaam:

We here in Moab have heard of your gift as a preacher. We want to engage you for some very special ministry. You will be expected to speak at least once in public. His Majesty, King Balak, will be present. Also, the king wants to consult you about a private matter.

On behalf of the king, may I acquaint you with the situation here in Moab? His Majesty has a problem directly connected with the nation of Israel. It is of the utmost importance that you keep this in mind.

Recently the Israelites have begun to come back to the promised land. This greatly upsets His Majesty. Their encampment is spoiling his view. The king is anxious to be assured from the Scriptures that there is no future for Israel as a nation. Therefore anything you can do to spiritualize the promises of Jehovah to Abraham, Isaac, and Jacob will be much appreciated here in Moab. On no account must you say anything about a literal fulfillment of these promises. Such an idea is abhorrent to Balak. I trust I have made myself clear.

Should you attempt to take the literal-cultural-grammatical approach to the question of Israel, you will incur the king's gravest displeasure. If that is your intention, it would be better for you not to come at all.

Your approach to the whole question of Israel must be strictly allegorical. In fact if you can emphasize that the sins, the unbelief, and the materialism of the present people of Israel militate against a literal fulfillment of God's promises to them, His Majesty will be well pleased.

The subject of the private session with the king will be salvation. I advise you in advance that His Majesty believes in salvation by works. He thinks that God must be propitiated by our own efforts. We want no cheap gospel here in Moab.

Now as to the honorarium. Our ambassador has been instructed to leave a large purse of gold with you to cover your traveling expenses. I assure you that should your preaching please His Highness, his liberality will be worthy of Moab. However, should you dare to present views that conflict with his, you will put yourself in danger. We have grim dungeons here in Moab and we know how to make a man wish he had never been born.

The king's business requires haste. Therefore please give your response to the king's ambassador.

Yours on behalf of His Highness,
*Ehud*
Imperial Secretary

God warned Balaam not to go to Moab. God told him that he would be better off not to preach at all than to tickle the ears of a wicked king. But Balaam was willing to preach contrary to the revealed word of God. All he could see was the fat honorarium promised by Balak. All Balaam could think of was the way his reputation would be enhanced if he preached for a king. So Balaam packed his bags and went to Moab.

We can picture the king greeting Balaam and then explaining the situation to him in detail. Balak wanted him to curse the Hebrew people, and Balaam was agreeable, as he had no particular love for Jews. But each time he tried to curse them, God seized his tongue—just as He had seized the tongue of the donkey—and forced him to bless them. And each time the king became more angry.

Balak's idea of viewing the Jews from different vantage

points did not help. Balaam simply was unable to curse them from the mountaintop. He was looking down on the Jews from above, seeing them as God saw them. In God's eyes they were perfect. God did not see their failings and imperfections; he saw them as they would be when He had finished with them. God's purposes and promises cannot fail.

## A. His Prophetic Preaching

In spite of himself, Balaam proclaimed the word of the Lord. Four words sum up Balaam's prophetic ministry in Moab. The first is *separation*. "The people shall dwell alone," Balaam said, "and shall not be reckoned among the nations…. Let me die the death of the righteous, and let my last end be like his!" (Numbers 23:9-10)

The second word is *justification*. Balaam told Balak, "[God] hath not beheld iniquity in Jacob, neither hath he seen perverseness in Israel: the Lord his God is with him, and the shout of a king is among them" (Numbers 23:21).

The third word is *sanctification*. Balaam prophesied, "How goodly are thy tents, O Jacob, and thy tabernacles, O Israel!… Blessed is he that blesseth thee, and cursed is he that curseth thee" (Numbers 24:5,9). The tents and tabernacle symbolized a pilgrim people who had no lasting roots down here and who were set apart for God (see Hebrews 11:8-10,13-16).

The fourth word is *exaltation*. Balaam foretold, "There shall come a Star out of Jacob, and a Sceptre shall rise out of Israel…. Out of Jacob shall come he that shall have dominion" (Numbers 24:17,19).

By the time Balaam had uttered all these prophecies, he was afraid for his life. The Moabite king was ready to have his hireling prophet hung, drawn, and quartered. So Balaam sought to pacify the king by whispering a suggestion in his ear that translated the whole situation from the realm of the spiritual into the realm of the sensual. "My lord," Balaam said in effect, "it's no use trying to curse the Jews from up here. Let's go down to where they are. Let's meet them on quite a different plane. Let's get down to the actual level on which they live. Then we will find a way to bring these prophecies to nothing."

## B. His Practical Preaching

Balaam's preaching on salvation is not recorded in the historical section of the Bible. It is tucked away in the book of the prophet Micah, who wrote centuries later. Evidently the Holy Spirit considered Balaam's message for Balak to be worth preserving. Balaam's gospel preaching would have done credit even to Peter or Paul.

In Micah 6:6-7 we read that Balak posed a question. In effect he asked, "What can I give the Most High so that He will overlook my sins?" Without waiting for Balaam's reply, he began to make bids, as if he were at an auction: "I will give burnt offerings, year-old calves, thousands of rams, rivers of oil, my firstborn son. I will give the fruit of my body for the sin of my soul. What does the Almighty think of that?"

Balaam had to tell the godless king the unpalatable truth that salvation cannot be bought or earned by performing good works or religious rites. Balak needed to understand what this verse of song acknowledges:

> Not the labors of my hands
> Can fulfill Thy law's demands;
> Could my zeal no respite know,
> Could my tears forever flow,
> All for sin could not atone;
> Thou must save and Thou alone.[1]

In effect Balaam declared to Balak, "Salvation is not for sale. Even if it were, it could not be purchased with the currency you are offering. Try a different medium of exchange. Here is what God demands: Do justly, love mercy, and walk humbly with God" (see Micah 6:8).

Since God demands a life of *transparent honesty,* Balaam

told Balak "to do justly." We can almost hear the preacher interrogating the king: "Have you always done unto others as you would have them do unto you? Have you always, without a single exception, lived a life beyond all possibility of recrimination or reproach? In all your wide circle of contacts, have you always done what was fair, right, good, just, and honest? Have you lived a life of absolute moral integrity?

Since God demands a life of *tender humanity,* Balaam advised Balak "to love mercy." If Balaam had heard the sermon on the mount, he would have quoted, "Blessed are the merciful," friend Balak, "for they shall obtain mercy" (Matthew 5:7). And if *The Merchant of Venice* had been written, Balaam would have recited:

> The quality of mercy is not strain'd,
> It droppeth as the gentle rain from heaven
> Upon the place beneath: it is twice bless'd;
> It blesseth him that gives and him that takes:
> 'Tis mightiest in the mightiest: it becomes
> The throned monarch better than his crown.[2]

"You hope to receive mercy," Balaam would have continued, "so offer God a life in which you have always showed mercy."

Since God demands a life of *true humility,* Balaam exhorted, "Walk humbly with thy God." We can almost hear Balaam dealing with Balak: "Have you walked with God, King Balak? Are you humble? Or are you as proud as Lucifer? Do you always esteem others better than yourself? If you want to merit eternal life, humility is God's price, Heaven's irreducible minimum. God can accept no less. If salvation could be purchased, justice, mercy, and humility would be the acceptable currency."

Balaam evidently knew more than most people about God's righteous demands. We are not told how Balak responded to his preaching.

# III. A VERY GRAVE PERIL

Balaam was in peril because he knew the truth of God and did nothing about it. He opened the door of the gospel for Balak with a flourish, but never went through that door himself. He said, "Let me die the death of the righteous" (Numbers 23:10), but he never lived the life of the righteous.

When he saw his honorarium flying away because of the king's rage over his preaching about the nation of Israel, Balaam came up with a lewd suggestion that had its source in his own unregenerate heart. "If you cannot curse them, my lord," he said in effect, "corrupt them. If you cannot conquer them with the men of Moab, seduce them with the women of Moab." (See Numbers 25; 31:16.) The Bible calls this suggestion "the doctrine of Balaam" (Revelation 2:14). The impact of Balaam's teaching is all too evident from the fact that he is mentioned ten times in the Bible outside of the book of Numbers.

How could such vileness coexist with such spiritual vision? It is possible to be in fellowship with the saints as Judas was, to fight the Lord's battles as Saul did, to desire to be prayed for as pharaoh did, to be baptized as Simon Magus was, to prophesy and speak of Christ as Caiaphas did, to evidence repentance and walk softly as Ahab did, to put away gross sin as Jehu did, to wish to die like the righteous as Balaam did— and still go to Hell!

What did Balaam do after he offered his sordid counsel to Balak? Instead of shaking the dust of Moab off his feet (see Luke 9:5) and going over to Israel's camp to meet Moses and seek God's salvation for himself, Balaam decided to return to his homeland. He collected his wages, packed his bags, then changed his mind and settled in Moab, where he met God's wrath shortly afterward at the hands of Joshua (Joshua 13:22).

The story of Balaam reminds us of the solemn warning found in Hebrews 10:26-29:

If we sin wilfully after that we have received the knowledge of the truth, there remaineth no more sacrifice for sins, But a certain fearful looking for of judgment.... He that despised Moses' law died without mercy under two or three witnesses: Of how much sorer punishment, suppose ye, shall he be thought worthy, who hath trodden under foot the Son of God, and hath counted the blood of the covenant, where-with he was sanctified, an unholy [valueless] thing, and hath done despite unto the Spirit of grace?

---

1. From the hymn "Rock of Ages" by Augustus M. Toplady.
2. Shakespeare, *The Merchant of Venice,* 4.1, Portia to Shylock.

# 9
# Joshua
# and His Victories

*Joshua 1–24*

The name *Joshua* in Hebrew has the same meaning as the name *Jesus* in Greek. In fact in Hebrews 4:8 the translators of the King James version substituted *Jesus* for *Joshua*. Both names mean "Jehovah is Savior."

# I. JOSHUA'S BACKGROUND

Joshua was born into the tribe of Ephraim, one of the most dominant tribes of Israel—second only to Judah. The spiritual heir of Moses, Joshua led the Hebrew people into Canaan.

We cannot help wondering what happened to Moses' sons. Did Moses fall so far short in his supreme duty as a father that he failed to bring up his sons properly? After Moses led the people out of Egypt, why did not Gershom or Eliezer step into their great father's footsteps and lead Israel on to victory?

We know that something went wrong because Gershom's son Jonathan acted as priest to the Danites when they set up a graven image for their tribe. The Hebrew custodians of the sacred Scriptures, who jealously guarded the integrity of the texts and used ingenious devices to preserve their pristine purity, seem to have deliberately changed the name of Jonathan's grandfather from Moses to Manasseh in Judges 18:30 to disguise the fact that Moses had such an outrageous descendant. No doubt the scribes thought that Moses would turn over in his grave if he knew what his grandson had done.

Often the family of a man of God do not recognize him as such, but other people do and they crowd around him. Gershom and Eliezer may have been aloof, but Joshua could always be found orbiting Moses. The young man felt the drawing power of Moses and came close to worshiping him.

Consider for instance the incident involving Eldad and Medad, who "prophesied in the camp" (Numbers 11:26-29). No doubt they were exceptional men, but Joshua was jealous of them on behalf of Moses. "My lord Moses, forbid them," he cried.

For years Moses had schooled his own heart against the sin of jealousy, so now the noble saint could simply reply, "Enviest thou for my sake? would God that all the Lord's people were prophets, and that the Lord would put his spirit upon them!" Thus Joshua was given a glimpse of the greatness of his hero.

When the Amalekites treacherously attacked Israel, Moses searched for a warrior he could leave in the valley to fight the physical foe while he went up to the mountain to fight the spiritual foe. It's no wonder that he selected his devoted follower Joshua. In effect Moses said, "Let me see what you can do with Amalek. I will uphold you in prayer." (See Exodus 17:8-16.)

In the typology of Scripture, Amalek represents the flesh at work in a violent way. We see "Amalek" in ourselves when we lose our temper, react angrily to a slight or an insult or an accusation, or when we attack somebody else. Victory over Amalek symbolizes victory over "the works of the flesh" in the power of the Holy Spirit (Galatians 5:10-26).

Moses chose Joshua again when he was sending twelve men to spy out the promised land. The excursion was invaluable training for a future leader. Joshua needed to experience the crossing of Jordan. He needed to be able to size up the foe. He needed to taste the fruit of Canaan.

And Joshua did not let Moses down. Although ten of the spies brought back an evil report, Joshua brought back a glowing report. All that the ten could see was the foe; all that Joshua could see was the fruit.

Thus Joshua was prepared by his background to become Moses' successor. He was prepared by *devotion*—by his commitment to God's man and all that he stood for among God's people and before the world. He was prepared by *discipline*—by subduing Amalek. And he was prepared by *duty*—by carrying out assignments with spiritual insight and courage, no matter how difficult or dangerous they were.

## II. JOSHUA'S BIBLE

When the mantle of Moses fell on Joshua, suddenly the full weight of responsibility was his. What should he do? Where could he turn? The older generation was gone. Those who had pioneered this great movement of God in the world were all dead. Moses, Aaron, Miriam, and Phinehas were gone. Only Joshua and Caleb remained.

The movement could not stand still. (Any movement that ceases to move is no longer a movement; it's a monument.) The next step was to cross Jordan. Surely Joshua wondered, *How am I supposed to move three million people to the other side of the river? How can I persuade so many to begin a new life of victory in the promised land? Moses sent twelve spies, but only Caleb and I appreciated Canaan.*

Joshua turned to the Word of God for answers, and this magnificent challenge from God came to his soul:

> This book of the law shall not depart out of thy mouth; but thou shalt meditate therein day and night, that thou mayest observe to do according to all that is written therein: for then thou shalt make thy way prosperous, and then thou shalt have good success (Joshua 1:8).

Joshua realized that he did not need Moses. He had what Moses had had: God's Word to guide him. With God's Word in his hand and in his heart, no situation could baffle him. No matter what he was called on to face, he would never have to be in doubt about what to do. All he needed to do was calmly search the Scriptures and govern his life by them. Joshua had a lamp unto his feet and a light unto his path (see Psalm 119:105). His own courage and wisdom would be inadequate for the struggles, situations, and strongholds he would have to face, but he would not be left to himself! He had the Bible.

And so do we. We should so saturate our souls with Scripture that we automatically and instinctively know God's mind concerning any matter that comes our way. God does not leave us to our own knowledge, understanding, or wisdom. We have "a more sure word of prophecy," as Peter put it, one to which we do well to "take heed, as unto a light that shineth in a dark place" (2 Peter 1:19).

# III. JOSHUA'S BELIEFS

Joshua matured quickly when he was forced to shoulder responsibility. That is not an uncommon phenomenon. I know a Christian lady who grew up overnight when she was suddenly widowed. Her husband had been a strong leader and steady Christian. She had leaned on him for everything—and rightly so. But when he was taken home to Heaven in the prime of life, she was left with the task of raising three little children by herself. Faced with this responsibility, she changed from a helpless clinging vine to a mature woman of the Word. She taught her children the Scriptures and nurtured them in a way that brought her credit down here and will earn her the Lord's "Well done!" at the judgment seat of Christ.

Joshua, as a spiritually mature leader, believed in a threefold vision of a new land, a new life, and a new Lord. His vision kept him true to God.

## A. A New Land

Canaan filled Joshua's vision. Having once been on the other side of Jordan, he longed for every man, woman, boy, and girl in Israel to cross that river too. Having once tasted the fruit of Canaan, he wanted everyone within the sphere of his influence to taste that fruit.

Some of God's people had suggested going back to Egypt, but that was not for Joshua. Egypt represented the world with all its pollution, perversions, politics, power, pleasures, prosperity, perspectives, prisons, pains, and prince. Joshua wanted no part of Egypt. He wanted Canaan! He longed for the promised land of milk and honey where God had put His name. He wanted Canaan with its battles and its blessings. He wanted Canaan, where the Israelites would find victory, peace, and glory.

## B. A New Life

When Joshua led God's people over Jordan, he placed twelve stones from the wilderness side of the river in the midst of the riverbed. After all the people arrived in the promised land, the first thing Joshua did was to build a memorial with twelve other stones that had been found in the riverbed. From then on, all the Israelites could point to the pillar and say, "This is where we crossed Jordan. This is where we died to the wilderness way of life with its disbelief, defeats, disasters, disappointments, and death. This is where we began our new life on the victory side of death." (See Joshua 4.)

Their new life, however, was made of sterner stuff than memorials and rites, no matter how sacred and Scriptural they might have been. Circumcision was required (Joshua 5:2-9). Circumcision spoke of the application of the cutting edge of the cross to the *flesh*. It was one thing to have entered into the victory of Christ's death, burial, and resurrection *positionally;* it was something else to have entered into it *practically*. Therefore Israel had to remove everything that represented the energy of the flesh. Before they could draw the sword on their foes, they had to draw the knife on themselves.

After the Israelites were circumcised, they kept the Passover (5:10). That spoke of their *faith*. They remembered that their new life had its roots in the death of the Passover lamb. If the people had forgotten that truth, they would not have been able to experience victorious living in Canaan. They were in the promised land by virtue of the sacrifice of the Passover lamb, which represented the coming death of Christ. Without that, they would still have been lost in Egypt.

Next the Israelites ate "the old corn of the land...and the manna ceased" (5:11-12). That spoke of the *future*. The manna was for the wilderness, for the wanderings, for the weak. The corn was for Canaan, for the battle, for the victory, for the strong. The manna represented Christ as the Bread of Heaven, the milk of the Word that God provided for His people while they were still carnal. The corn represented Christ as the food for His "grown-up" people. The manna had been sufficient while the Israelites were sojourners, but they needed corn in order to be soldiers.

## C. A New Lord

One day when Joshua was wondering how the Israelites would ever be able to scale the massive walls of Jericho, a man holding a drawn sword suddenly appeared. Joshua challenged him: "Art thou for us, or for our adversaries?" (Joshua 5:13). In other words, "Whose side are you on?"

"Nay; but as captain of the host of the Lord am I now come," the man replied (5:14).

Joshua instantly recognized that he was in the presence of the Lord of hosts, the living Christ Himself, and he flung himself at His feet. All the weight of responsibility shifted from Joshua's shoulders to the mighty shoulders of the Lord. The battle wasn't Joshua's; it was the Lord's. All Joshua had to do was trust and obey. He rose to his feet with his burden lifted. Victory was sure, for the Lord had taken command!

Joshua based his beliefs on the facts regarding a new land, a new life, and a new Lord. We too can stake everything on these facts—only our Canaan is a heavenly one, not an earthly promised land. When we cross our Jordan, we enter the heavenlies, where all our battles and our blessings are, as Paul's Epistle to the Ephesians tells us (1:3,20-23; 2:6; 6:11-13).

# IV. JOSHUA'S BATTLES

Joshua came to grips with four kinds of foes in Canaan. They represent the various foes that we must face if we intend to possess in a practical way those things which we already possess positionally by virtue of our identification with Christ.

## A. Major Foes

Jericho is an example of Joshua's major foes. One of the great walled cities of the promised land, Jericho stood squarely across Joshua's path. Not a step could he take without first dealing with Jericho. Failure here would mean failure everywhere.

Like Joshua, the believer in our day cannot rule over a kingdom he has not subdued. No sooner does he stake his claim in the death, burial, and resurrection of Christ and all the means of grace God has provided than he discovers in his path a major obstacle to a holy life. That obstacle has to be dealt with first. It may be an enslaving habit, a set of godless friends, a besetting sin, a temperamental weakness, an unsaved girl-friend, or a mean boss. Whatever the obstacle is, it stands in the way of further spiritual progress. This major foe will test whether or not he really means to go all the way with God.

Note how Joshua dealt with Jericho. (See Joshua 6.) First he acknowledged the lordship of Christ by submitting to the man with the drawn sword. After this *decisive experience,* he engaged in a *daily exercise* of obedience. Joshua did not attempt to deal with Jericho himself. It was not his resolve, his resistance, or his resources that brought victory. It was a case of "trust and obey." Day by day he simply walked around Jericho. Joshua obeyed because he had a *definite expectancy.* Hebrews 11:30 says that "by faith the walls of Jericho fell down." Joshua dared to believe that God would sweep away this obstacle as long as he was willing to cooperate with Him.

B. Minor Foes

After the victory at Jericho came the devastating defeat at Ai. Compared with Jericho, Ai was just a little city, but Joshua acted in the flesh when he attempted to take Ai. He made decisions without prayer or guidance from God's Word and he was ignominiously defeated. Likewise, after a believer has won a great spiritual victory, the first big temptation he faces is to imagine that although he needs God for the major foes, he can manage the minor foes without Him.

If Joshua had spent time with God before attacking Ai, God would have guided him and he would have saved himself from a humiliating loss. And today if people who are engaged in what passes for the Lord's work would spend time with God and His Word, their efforts would not be doomed to failure.

God had explicitly decreed that all the spoils of Jericho were His and that they were to be placed in His treasury. (See Joshua 6:18-19.) But Achan, a man in Joshua's army, had stolen some of the spoils and hidden them in his tent. Until this secret sin was exposed and judged, God's people could not be victorious at Ai or anywhere else. (See Joshua 7:1-12). Similarly one individual's unconfessed and uncleansed secret sin can affect the corporate life of the whole body of believers.

## C. Moderate Foes

One of Joshua's moderate foes used outright deception. (See Joshua 9–11.) Pretending to have come from a distant land (see Deuteronomy 20:10-16), the people of Gibeon offered Joshua an alliance and promised to submit to his rule. The proofs offered seemed genuine, so again Joshua acted independently of God. Without seeking divine guidance, he made peace with the Gibeonites. Soon Joshua discovered that he had been deceived. Gibeon was not far away; it was the next land slated for destruction by Israel. God made Joshua live with his treaty and it cost Israel dearly later on (2 Samuel 21:1-9).

Some mistakes we make today are like Joshua's mistake in his dealings with the Gibeonites. We marry out of the will of God, for example, or take a job that requires us to compromise with God's Word. Such mistakes can be costly, for often God makes us live with the consequences.

## D. Multiplied Foes

Sometimes when it seems as if everything is going wrong, as if our whole world is caving in, we are tempted to panic and think that God has abandoned us. In Joshua's case there were two times when everyone seemed to be conspiring against Israel.

On the first occasion a strong coalition of southern kings joined forces against Joshua. God helped him then in a way that illustrates the *providential* side of a spiritual victory. We read:

> The Lord cast down great stones from heaven upon
> them.... They were more which died with hailstones
> than they whom the children of Israel slew with the
> sword.... And the sun stood still, and the moon stayed
> until the people had avenged themselves upon their
> enemies (Joshua 10:11-13).

God simply stepped in, in a spectacular and supernatural way, and crushed the enemy. There could be no doubt that God had won this obviously miraculous victory.

Many of us know of similar instances of divine intervention. People have been suddenly, supernaturally, and surely delivered from alcohol, drugs, or tobacco. At a critical moment, a leader of the opposition has died or moved away. An unexpected check has arrived in the mail. Someone has come forward with new evidence. A door has opened or closed, dramatically changing the whole situation. Most missionaries can tell such stories, and the life of George Muller was full of such incidents. Sometimes God provides miraculous deliverances.

On the second occasion Joshua faced a coalition of his northern enemies. This time God helped Joshua in a way that illustrates the *personal* side of a spiritual victory. Throughout Joshua 11 we see the army of Israel smiting the opposition with the sword until every foe was subdued. God was fighting for the Israelites, but He provided no supernatural signs. They had matured and no longer needed miracles. They had learned how to handle the sword.

Many of us have known believers who struggled with besetting sins. They longed for and prayed for the supernatural deliverance that someone else had received, but no miracle happened to them. Instead God allowed them to live with their problems, to fight against their temptations in daily fierce encounters. God made them use His Word—the sword of the Spirit—against their sins.

As we mature spiritually, God makes us rely increasingly

on the Bible. He wants us to bring the cutting edge of His Word to bear on the things in our lives that hold us back from victory. We would rather see God's spectacular intervention; God would rather see us study Scripture.

## V. JOSHUA'S BRETHREN

When Joshua realized that his life was almost over, he "gathered all the tribes of Israel to Shechem, and called for the elders of Israel" (Joshua 24:1). The name *Shechem* means "strength," so he was summoning the people to the place of strength. There he challenged them: "Choose you this day whom ye will serve.... As for me and my house, we will serve the Lord" (24:15). God's people were in danger of being ensnared by new idols, so Joshua warned them, "Put away...the strange gods which are among you, and incline your heart unto the Lord God of Israel" (24:23).

Joshua had blazed the trail for the Israelites. He had taught them the principles of spiritual victory and had lived victoriously before them, but he could not live for them. They had to choose the victory side. Joshua had made his choice years earlier when he had given his wholehearted support to Moses. He had made a commitment to trust and obey God and he had stood by that commitment. Joshua had brought up his family to trust and obey and he urged all Israel to live by that principle. If he were living today, he would say:

> When we walk with the Lord in the light of His Word,
> What a glory He sheds on our way!
> While we do His good will He abides with us still,
> And with all who will trust and obey.
>
> Trust and obey, for there's no other way
> To be happy in Jesus,
> But to trust and obey.
>
> (John H. Sammis)

# 10
# Eli
# and His Faults

*1 Samuel 1–4*

---

I. ELI'S FAILURE AS A PRIEST
    A.  No Spiritual Vision
    B.  No Spiritual Vitality
    C.  No Spiritual Values

II. ELI'S FAILURE AS A PARENT
    A.  Eli's Sons Were Unregenerate
    B.  Eli's Sons Were Unrestrained
    C.  Eli's Sons Were Unrepentant

---

Eli was a priest, a descendant of Aaron through his fourth and youngest son Ithamar. The name *Eli* means "God is high." So every time his name was spoken, every time he signed his name, Eli was reminded that he was a servant of the highest of masters, that he was called and consecrated to the highest of all occupations. My father used to say, "Think great thoughts of God!" One could not have a greater concept of God than the concept enshrined in Eli's name.

It is more of an honor to be one of the Lord's servants than to be the son of a king. A person involved in the ministry of the Most High has a nobler task than he who rules an empire. God's "prince," Jacob, was a greater man than Egypt's king. When

Joseph presented his father to the pharaoh, "Jacob blessed Pharaoh." Pharaoh only had power with men; Jacob had power with God. (See Genesis 32:28; 47:10).

In spite of his high-sounding name, Eli failed as a priest and as a parent. As a result, tragedy cast its dark shadow on his life. Some tragedies can be avoided, yet we see them all about us today—in our churches, in our homes, in our society, and in the world at large. Perhaps the story of Eli will help us avoid some of life's pitfalls and preventable tragedies.

# I. ELI'S FAILURE AS A PRIEST

Eli failed as a priest in three critical ways. He lost his spiritual vision, his spiritual vitality, and his spiritual values. No wonder there was no victory or joy among God's people. No wonder the rank and file were a prey to their enemies. Their leader was in a backslidden condition. Eli had lost sight of the significance of his name and was content to live in the lowlands of life.

## A. No Spiritual Vision

"The word of the Lord was precious [rare][1] in those days; there was no open vision.... [Eli's] eyes began to wax dim, that he could not see" (1 Samuel 3:1-2).

The first time we meet Eli (in 1 Samuel 1), his lack of spiritual insight is apparent. A brokenhearted woman named Hannah had come up to the tabernacle to pray about the barrenness of her life. She desperately wanted to be fruitful for God. Indeed much of the book of Samuel hinges on her absolute refusal to take no for an answer. She was determined to have the blessing of God. As she earnestly poured out her soul to the Lord, her lips moved but her prayer was silent. Eli, seeing her lips moving, concluded that she was drunk and sharply reprimanded her. When he discovered his mistake, he half apologized by offering her his worthless blessing.

Eli had no spiritual vision. The Bible says, "Where there is no vision, the people perish" (Proverbs 29:18). That proverb was true then and it is true today. It is a serious situation when Christians have no spiritual vision. Things are happening in our world that make the angels weep, but some of us are so shortsighted or so preoccupied with personal matters that we cannot see other people's needs even when they are brought to our attention.

Let's look at the world with its needs and resources. First let us consider our own country. Americans own disproportionate percentages of the world's cars; hospital beds; bathtubs; radio, telegraph, and telephone facilities; life insurance policies; and wealth. Yet we occupy only 6 percent of the world's land and comprise only 7 percent of the world's population.

Now let us consider the world in general. About 180 years ago, it was estimated that Protestant Christians made up 25 percent of the known world's population. Today only 8 percent can be classified as such. By the year 2000 it is estimated that only 2 percent of the world's population will be Protestant Christians. There will be six billion people in the world (three billion of them in Asia) and 98 percent of all the people on the planet will be in spiritual darkness. "Where there is no vision, the people perish"!

There are 5,690 known languages in the world. A Bible or New Testament has been published in only 746 of these languages. There are 3,483 languages into which no portion of the Word of God has been translated. "Where there is no vision, the people perish"!

During the period of missionary expansion, the three major non-Christian religions (Islam, Buddhism, and Hinduism) put up a more or less passive resistance to the gospel. Now these three religions are actively resistant. Totally rejecting the gospel of Christ, they have become militant and confident that they are now in a position not merely to resist Christianity, but to replace it altogether.

Today's educated Hindu is as comfortable in New York, London, or Paris as he is in Bombay and feels as much at home in the world of advanced medicine, high technology, modern engineering, or international finance as the Christian does. The Hindu moves freely in the modern world without casting off the moorings of his Hindu faith. He will acknowledge that modern Hinduism owes something to Christianity, but he will quickly tell you that most of what the gospel has brought to light is a forgotten part of the original Hindu tradition. Western civilization has only served to remind him of these ideas.

Hindus, Muslims, and Buddhists are quite sure that the period during which Christian nations had their chance for world leadership is over. All three feel that nations responsible for producing the atomic bomb and the pornographic movie have nothing to say to them. They are convinced that Christianity is a farce and a failure and that if the West insists that its moral superiority gives it the right to preach to the rest of the world, it will be laughed out of court.

Hinduism, Islam, and Buddhism are experiencing a renaissance. Their devotees are determined to spread their philosophies in western lands and zealously seek converts among the youth on our college campuses. The wealthy Arab states of OPEC are pouring billions of dollars into the conversion of black Africa to Islam. Islamic fundamentalism has become a power to be reckoned with. Buddhists say that communism was an outgrowth of Christianity. They are bold, aggressive, and out to spread the word that Buddha is the true savior of the world; they use newspapers, magazines, radio, television, tracts, and all the modern methods of evangelism in their efforts to convert the Far East to Buddha. The cults of Christendom, likewise, are on the march. They are aggressive, mobilized, zealous, wealthy, and growing.

In the meantime most Christians are content to come and go to meetings. Many settle for a Sunday-morning-only compromise with conscience and Christ. They pour their money into material things and spend their time improving their financial position or having fun. They shut their eyes to a lost world. Like Eli, they have no spiritual vision and "where there is no vision, the people perish."

## B. No Spiritual Vitality

Scripture portrays Eli as old and tired. Conditions among his people were deplorable, yet he could not be bothered to stir himself to take action. *If people want the truth,* he seemed to think, *let them come to me. Why should I go to them? I have done my share. It's time somebody else got busy.*

We meet Eli three times in the Old Testament. The first time we see him sitting down, propped up by a post in the tabernacle (1 Samuel 1:9). The second time we see him in bed, sound asleep, and God had to talk to a little boy. Indeed young Samuel had to wake Eli up three times to tell him that somebody was calling (1 Samuel 3). The last time Eli appears, we see him sitting on a seat by the wayside. He hears that the Philistines have captured the ark and falls off that seat only to break his neck and die (1 Samuel 4:13-18). Eli had no spiritual vitality.

Many of us are just like Eli, unwilling to stir ourselves, unwilling to get busy. The majority of professing Christians do not want to get involved or make any commitments that might tie them down. They want to be footloose and fancy-free. They want to be at liberty to hop from one church to another, to go to an early Sunday service and then head for the lake. Most are scared to death to take on anything that requires self-sacrificing discipline. Content with a secondhand faith and a peripheral knowledge of the Bible, they have no spiritual vitality.

Another look at the world will reveal the need for spiritual vitality on the missionfield. Consider India, one of the most strategically important countries in terms of world evangelism. Its population is twice that of the thirty major countries of Africa combined. Many of India's 936 million people are wedded to the gross superstitions and idolatries of Hinduism. The country has fourteen major languages and more than seven hundred dialects. India touches the great Muslim world that stretches from Indonesia to the Atlantic; it is close to Russia and China; and the Buddhist states of Sri Lanka, Burma, and Thailand are on its doorstep. Yet India has scarcely been evangelized.

India needs a modern-day Paul. Paul made an astonishing

statement in Romans 15:19: "From Jerusalem, and round about
unto Illyricum, I have fully preached the gospel of Christ." The
apostle was claiming to have fully evangelized an area stretch-
ing through Syria, across Asia Minor into Macedonia and
Greece, and up the Adriatic into present-day Yugoslavia. He
took a mere fifteen years to evangelize the cities and populated
areas on a route that was over fifteen hundred miles long! Paul
did not accomplish that feat by sitting around daydreaming or
by wishful thinking.

Think of it: fifteen hundred miles! A line that long would
stretch all the way from New York City to Dallas, Texas. In India
the line would extend from Bombay up to Delhi and across to
Calcutta. It would have taken Paul three months just to travel
that distance, even if he used the magnificent Roman roads.

Paul's claim to have fully evangelized that vast area does
not mean that he personally spoke to every individual along the
way. It means that he planted a church in every major city along
the route. Because he fired those churches with his own tireless
zeal for expansion, he could honestly say that that part of the
world had been completely saturated with the gospel.

Paul, who was a young man when Stephen was martyred,
began his new life in Christ in A.D. 36 and died a martyr in A.D.
68. He was called to the missionfield in A.D. 45. So he was a
Christian for about thirty-two years and a missionary for twenty-
three (including the years he spent in prison). He is held up to
us by the Holy Spirit as a model Christian who could challenge
the community of believers with these words: "Be ye followers
of me, even as I also am of Christ" (1 Corinthians 11:1). Few of
us would care to make such a statement. What spiritual vitality
Paul had! In contrast, Eli had none.

C. No Spiritual Values

God sent Eli a warning in which He said, "[Thou] honourest
thy sons above me" (1 Samuel 2:29). Somehow or other, Eli's values
had become all mixed up. Eli had allowed the interests of his
godless sons to take precedence over the interests of God's people.

Whenever we allow family, business, pleasure, or education to usurp God's place, our spiritual values become distorted. We become so complacent that we can sit back and watch the church go to ruin. We can let the world hurry on its way toward a Christless eternity and excuse ourselves for doing nothing.

Amy Wilson Carmichael was a missionary with a good sense of values. She went to Japan and Ceylon and finally settled in southern India, where she stayed for thirty-five consecutive years. She devoted herself to rescuing girls from lives of servitude and prostitution in Hindu temples. Amy related how God convicted her and transformed her into a tireless worker:

She fell into a fitful sleep one night, a sleep disturbed by the beating of the native tom-toms at a local pagan festival. In her dream she saw a chasm that gaped deep and wide. Hurrying toward that abyss were thousands of people of all ages and classes. They pressed forward, heedless of the peril ahead. As they reached the gulf, one by one they toppled into it. Their cries haunted her. Then she noticed that all of the people were blind. Here and there along the top of the chasm stood a couple or a lone man or woman who could see. They were working hard to warn the other people, but met with little success. The chasm was so vast and the workers were so few. Then Amy noticed a group sitting under a tree nearby. Not being blind, they knew about the gulf, but they were too busy making daisy chains to help dissuade the multitudes.

When she awoke, the drummers were still beating their tom-toms and the cries of devil dancers were still ringing through the darkness. But the voice of God thundered even more loudly in her soul. He was asking, "What hast *thou* done?"

For Amy Carmichael, that dream settled the whole question of values once and for all.

Eli failed miserably as a priest. His failure should prompt us to ask ourselves how we are doing in this age when all believers are priests. Each of us has a ministry. Each of us has been anointed by the Holy Spirit for the work of God and each has received "the mighty ordination of the pierced hands." Are we fulfilling the ministries God has put into our hands?

## II. ELI'S FAILURE AS A PARENT

We cannot divorce one of Eli's failures from the other altogether. His sons Hophni and Phinehas saw so much that was inconsistent in both the life and ministry of their father. They saw his lackadaisical attitude toward the things of God. From him they imbibed low views of the priesthood. Eli thrust his sons into the Lord's work even though they were wholly unfit for it. Looking on the ministry as a comfortable, convenient way to earn a living, Hophni and Phinehas were out to enjoy the power and prestige that the priesthood bestowed.

The Holy Spirit tells us that Eli's sons were unregenerate, unrestrained, and unrepentant.

### A. Eli's Sons Were Unregenerate

First Samuel 2:12 says, "The sons of Eli were sons of Belial." We would say, "They were children of the devil." That is strong language. Scripture goes on to say, "They knew not the Lord." In other words, Hophni and Phinehas were unregenerate. Yet they were in the ministry because their father hoped that some of the holiness of their office might rub off on their lives. Eli hoped in vain. His sons were wolves in sheep's clothing, false pastors of God's flock.

Of course it is not always the father's fault when children do not accept Christ. The fact that they are born into a godly home does not guarantee that they will be saved. They have a better chance than other children and are a great deal more accountable than other children, but their salvation is not automatic.

I am reminded of the question a godly father asked me one day. A brave old warrior who had done pioneer missionary work in the Yukon, he was faithful and tireless in soulwinning, but his son, who was already in his thirties, was unsaved. The father asked, "Why do you think God doesn't answer my prayer for my son?"

I replied, "I don't know why."

"Well," he continued, "some years ago God spoke to me about my unsaved son. 'I'm going to save your son,' He said, 'but for now I want you to have an unsaved son so that you will be able to feel for others who have unsaved sons!'"

That was not the reason in Eli's case, however. The fact that his children were "sons of Belial" is noted right along with his own failure as a priest. Eli's indifference toward God's family had direct repercussions in his own family.

## B. Eli's Sons Were Unrestrained

The Holy Spirit tells us the whole terrible tale. The vile sons of Eli used their position in the priesthood to take advantage of the women who came to them with spiritual needs (1 Samuel 2:22). Eli, who had never disciplined his rebellious sons when they were young, found that now when he wished to restrain them, he could not.

When Eli heard about the immoral lives Hophni and Phinehas were living and about their scorn for the Word of God, he wrung his hands and compromised. When God warned him that he would not escape accountability for his sons' wicked behavior, the indulgent old man contented himself with a mild reproof. Even though his sons were guilty of utter contempt for the things of God, he did not evict them from the priesthood or excommunicate them from the faith. Licentious in behavior and liberal in belief, they still posed as priests of God.

## C. Eli's Sons Were Unrepentant

Hophni and Phinehas simply shrugged their shoulders at their father's rebuke. "They hearkened not," commented the Holy Spirit (1 Samuel 2:25). At that point their case passed from human hands to God's hands. He took over and met those two men in judgment. There was no escape from the sentence and no court of appeal. Eli was judged at the same time.

What a failure poor old Eli was! But something can be said in his favor. He served as the high priest of Israel even though the high priesthood belonged to a different branch of Aaron's family. Somehow Eli stood in the gap that a more qualified man should have filled. The job was too big for Eli; the times were too evil. We can be sure that when God judges Eli, He who is fair as well as forgiving will take this service into account.

And although Eli failed with his sons, he did a remarkable job of bringing up little Samuel. Hannah promised to give Samuel to God, and the only way she knew how to do that was to give him to Eli. She bathed the whole situation in prayer and entrusted her boy to the high priest's care. Thus Eli received a second chance.

He so recovered himself as priest and parent that when he died, he left Israel with a spiritual giant: Samuel, who became the last of the judges and the first of the prophets. Samuel in turn left Israel with David and a signpost pointing directly ahead to Christ.

It is never too late to be rescued from a life of failure. If we learn the bitter lessons of our failures, submit ourselves to the mighty hand of God, walk softly before Him, and seek to be diligent in some area of service, the Lord will bless us.

When Eli received his second chance, he might well have said: "This one thing I do. Forgetting those things which are behind, I press forward toward the mark and toward the prize. I will take this child and make a believer, a saint, and a prophet out of him." And so he did.

---

1. The Hebrew word translated "precious" literally means "heavy" (in price). There are five "precious" things in the Old Testament: God's word (1 Samuel 3:1); redemption (Psalm 49:8); the death of God's saints (Psalm 72:14; 116:15); the lips of knowledge (Proverbs 20:15); and the thoughts of God (Psalm 139:17).

Instead of God's people taking the lead in the world, the world was pouring God's people into its mold.

The same sad conditions prevail in much of the church today. We have become so accustomed to defeat and so acclimatized to disorganization and declension that we accept them as the norm. Most of us are far more astonished when somebody is saved in one of our services than we are when nobody is saved. Yet conversions should be as common as birthdays.

We have become used to the fact that our children are bored with our services and do not share our convictions. We are not surprised that we have to fight with our young people to get them to come to church. When we see them march defiantly into the world, we just accept it and say, "Well, we did our best. It's not our fault. It's the spirit of the age."

First Samuel begins in a day as dark as ours. The priesthood was corrupt and the high priest was a feeble old man who should have retired years earlier. Eli had placed his sons in the ministry in spite of the fact that their public and private lives were scandalous. Israel was a picture of Thyatiran apostasy and Laodicean apathy. Her people were demoralized and depressed and her enemies were oppressive.

Into this scene the Holy Spirit brought a remarkable godly woman named Hannah. Thank God for all the women like Hannah whom God has raised up over the years! Susanna Wesley is an example. She was the mother of nineteen children, two of whom—John and Charles—were instrumental in leading England back to God. Susanna was their first teacher. She laid such a solid foundation of Bible knowledge in their souls that all their subsequent ministries were built upon it.

Susanna's husband Samuel was a fiery preacher. The people of his parish were a profligate crowd and when Samuel admonished them sharply for their sins, they set his house on fire. Several of his children clambered through a downstairs window; others escaped through a side door; Susanna waded through a wall of flames to safety. But six-year-old John was left behind in the excitement. His father heard him crying in the upstairs nursery but could not reach him because the stairs had collapsed. The little boy climbed up on a chest by the window, and two brave peasants—one standing on the shoulders of the other—plucked John out of the conflagration just as the window fell in. In later years he often referred to himself as "a brand plucked from the burning."

The life of Charles was also remarkably preserved. He was born prematurely and the attendants thought he was dead because he neither opened his eyes nor cried. For some time he gave no signs of life, but then his mother thought she detected a faint heartbeat. She wrapped the infant in soft wool and kept him warm for several weeks. When the moment came when he should have been born, had he not been delivered prematurely, he opened his eyes, cried, and behaved in every way like a normal newborn baby.

John and Charles Wesley both felt that they were destined to be used of God. They were born in an age that needed a mighty moving of the Spirit in revival. Historians agree that conditions were never darker in England than they were prior to the coming of the Wesleyan revival.

The theater was decadent. The royal court and the castles of the nobility reeked with licentiousness. The people scorned religion and devoured the atheistic writings of Hume, Gibbon, and Voltaire. Drunkenness was widespread.

In 1736, just three years before the Methodist revival began, every sixth house in London was a gin mill. The signboards of these public houses advertised that they would make a man drunk for a penny and dead drunk for two. They would also provide a free bed on which a man could sleep off his stupor and a morning dram of gin with which to ease his hangover. From these establishments, gangs of thieves sallied forth to outrage the community, kill, maim, torture, and perform all kinds of atrocities.

The universities and colleges seethed with atheism and radical philosophies. The priests of the Anglican church were, for the most part, worldly men. Augustus Toplady, who wrote the hymn "Rock of Ages," said that a converted Anglican minister "was as great a wonder as a comet."[1] The bishop of Litchfield said: "The Lord's day is now the devil's market day. More lewdness, more drunkenness, more quarrels and murders, more sin, is contrived and committed on this day than on all the other days of the week together."[2]

Rampant immorality was openly defended and justified. Virtually every kind of sin found a writer to teach it and a bookseller to spread it. Bishop Butler said that it was taken for granted that Christianity was no longer a subject for inquiry.

England in the eighteenth century sorely needed revival just as Israel needed revival in the twelfth century B.C. God sent England a Susanna Wesley, and Israel a Hannah. Would that today He would send America and England another Hannah or Susanna!

As we consider Hannah's story, we will see that it progresses from barrenness, bitterness, and brokenness to blessedness.

# I. BARRENNESS

> Now there was a certain man of Ramathaim-zophim, of mount Ephraim, and his name was Elkanah.... And he had two wives; the name of the one was Hannah, and the name of the other Peninnah: and Peninnah had children, but Hannah had no children (1 Samuel 1:1-2).

Let us look first at Hannah's husband. He was a Levite— that is, he was from the tribe of Israel that God had set apart to minister His Word to the people. There were three Levitical families and Elkanah came from the most distinguished of the three: the family of Kohath, to which Moses and Aaron had belonged. The descendants of Kohath were entrusted with the most important ministry in the service of the tabernacle. Their task was to carry in their hands the ark, the lampstand, the table, and the golden altar when Israel was on the march. The rest of the furniture and fittings of the tabernacle were carried on carts.

Elkanah lived at Ramathaim-zophim. The name of the town is said to mean "the two hills of the watchman." Every time Elkanah wrote or spoke the name, he was reminded of the need for watchfulness. Again and again the Bible warns us to be constantly on guard against the perils and pitfalls of life, against Satan's snares and traps.

The fact that Elkanah had two wives is silent but eloquent proof of his lack of watchfulness. Although the Mosaic law permitted polygamy, God never really blessed it. The system never bred happiness, just discord and dissension.

Years ago a *Reader's Digest* article on Chinese picture writing showed some of the ideograms used to convey ideas in that language. Each example was a combination of the character for *woman* and the character for some thought associated with *woman*. The character for *woman* plus the character for *child* combine to form the word *lovely*. The character for *woman* plus the character for *roof* combine to form the ideogram for *peace*. To the Chinese a picture of a woman under a roof conveys the idea of peace. On the other hand, two of the character for *woman* combine to form the ideogram for *quarrel*. Two of the character for *woman* drawn under the character for *roof* form the ideogram for *trouble*. The cynic would say that two women under one roof is trouble in any language!

Having two wives certainly created trouble in Elkanah's home. He loved Hannah more than he loved Peninnah and as a result his domestic life was stressful.

Turning our attention to the wives, we note that Peninnah was fruitful, but Hannah was barren. That is hard to understand. Why should Hannah, the more spiritual of the two, be unfruitful? Peninnah was carnal, spiteful, cantankerous, mean, and small-minded. Why should she be fruitful? We cannot explain why she had the children.

As we consider this situation, we can see parallels in the spiritual realm. We cannot always explain fruitfulness or barrenness in our churches. We cannot explain why revival has broken out in so many Third World countries while the Muslim world remains an unproductive field. We cannot always explain why God blesses one man's ministry with souls but not another's. The apparent lack of blessing does not necessarily mean that the first man is more spiritual than the second.

Years ago a friend of mine became the pastor of a church that was torn by dissension. Only fifty people were left in what had once been a thriving congregation. He built that church up to a membership of more than two hundred in less than a year. What amazed me was that he often telephoned me on a Saturday night and asked me to give him a sermon outline. He would use that outline in the pulpit the next morning and a dozen people would come forward for salvation. When I preached from that same outline, I rarely saw anyone come forward.

I once heard a famous evangelist preach a message that contained little or no substance. The sermon was insipid and disorganized. The brief introductory remarks were of a general nature relating to current events, the illustrations were few and poor, the outline was barely discernible, and the style of delivery was cold. The message—really just a series of assertions—was true to the Bible, but would have received barely a passing grade in a homiletics class! Yet when the evangelist made the appeal, people marched forward by the thousands to seek salvation.

We cannot always explain barrenness and fruitfulness. All we know is that God is sovereign and He is answerable to no one. "The wind bloweth where it listeth," the Holy Spirit says. "So is every one that is born of the Spirit" (John 3:8).

Returning to the story of Hannah, we find no explanation for Hannah's barrenness. We can say, however, that Hannah's child, when she finally had one, was worth a hundred children Peninnah might have had. Not one of Peninnah's children, as far as we know, amounted to anything for God, but Hannah's little boy became God's answer to an apostate, apathetic age.

# II. BITTERNESS

Peninnah "provoked [Hannah] sore, for to make her fret" (1 Samuel 1:6). In other words, Hannah became upset by her lack of fruit. Her reaction was natural, but it did no good at all. Likewise we will never see God move in our midst if the extent of our concern is just idle regret because others (even those whose doctrine is not nearly as sound as ours) are seeing results and we are not.

Then Hannah wept. That was a better reaction! We can make another spiritual application of the story here, for the Bible says, "He that goeth forth and weepeth, bearing precious seed, shall doubtless come again with rejoicing, bringing his sheaves with him" (Psalm 126:6). When was the last time we saw tears shed in a meeting because no souls were being saved? When was the last time we parents cried real tears because our children had no interest in the things of God? Perhaps God is waiting for us to be more genuinely concerned. Perhaps He is waiting for our tears.

Have we, in all our years, ever known a church to call a special series of meetings in order to fast and pray for souls? Hannah, we read in 1 Samuel 1:7, "did not eat." Have we ever gone without a meal ourselves to show God our utter desperation and earnestness about those we wish to see saved?

Returning to the story line, we note that while Hannah prayed in the house of the Lord, "Eli the priest sat upon a seat by a post of the temple of the Lord" (1:9). The acknowledged leader of God's people was so utterly unconcerned, so spiritually indolent, so downright lazy and indifferent that he could plop down at ease while nearby a woman wept out her heart over her barrenness. What kind of a pastor was he?

Eli failed her, but God didn't. All Hannah's troubles, all her barrenness and bitterness, were designed by God to drive her in desperation to Himself. Perhaps Samuel would not have been born if Peninnah had been kind to Hannah. God used Peninnah's acid tongue and spiteful disposition to accomplish His will.

# III. BROKENNESS

"[Hannah] was in bitterness of soul, and prayed unto the Lord" (1 Samuel 1:10). There is something remarkable about Hannah's prayer: for the first time in Scripture the name translated "Lord" is *Jehovah Sabaoth,* which means "the Lord of warrior hosts."

This title is not found in the Pentateuch or in the books of Joshua or Judges. Jeremiah, the weeping prophet, used it about eighty times and the postexilic prophets, in days of danger and disappointment, used the name about ninety times. It was reserved, however, for this godly woman to use it for the first time. In effect, she cried out:

> Oh Lord of warrior hosts! Think of all the heavenly hosts You have. Think of the angels, archangels, cherubim, seraphim, and countless sons of light. Think of these mighty warrior hosts on high who hang on Your words and rush to do Your bidding. Think too of Your human warrior hosts. Think, Lord, of the thousands of Israelites! Think of all those who have already run their course. Lord, You have so many. Spare me one, just one, Oh Lord. But not just anyone. Let me bring one of Your crisis men into the world. Give me a son who will grow up to be a warrior and win victories for the people of God. Lord, I'd rather have one son like that than a hundred sons who amount to nothing.

As Hannah prayed, "she vowed a vow, and said, O Lord of hosts, if thou wilt...give unto thine handmaid a man child, then I will give him unto the Lord all the days of his life, and there shall no razor come upon his head" (1:11). In other words she was promising, "If you give me a baby boy, I'll see to it that he grows up to be a warrior for You. I'll begin, Lord, by making a Nazarite out of him."

A Nazarite was not allowed to cut his hair, drink wine, or touch any dead body—not even that of his nearest and dearest. His appearance, his appetites, and his affections were all to be laid on the altar. The Nazarite vow was normally temporary, but there are three lifelong Nazarites in Scripture: Samson, John the Baptist, and Samuel.

Hannah pledged herself to train her boy to be a lifelong Nazarite, wholly set apart for God. She made a commitment to school that little fellow so effectively that for the rest of his days he would live with a consuming passion for God. She would bend the twig so that the fully grown tree would lean forever toward God. That was a tremendous commitment for her as well as for the son she craved.

We note Hannah's brokenness in the presence of God and the priest's evaluation of her condition. "You're drunk," Eli said in effect. The same evaluation was given by the people of Jerusalem when they saw the apostles filled with the Holy Spirit on the day of Pentecost.

"No, my lord," Hannah softly replied (1:15). How Christlike she was. She reminds us of Him "who, when he was reviled, reviled not again" (1 Peter 2:23).

"Go in peace," said Eli (1 Samuel 1:17). That was the worthless blessing of an empty old man who had spent his life in the Lord's work without power or spiritual profit. This dear and desperate woman had more power with God in fifty-five words of prayer than the old minister had during fifty-five years and more as priest and judge.

# IV. BLESSEDNESS

Hannah knew that God had answered her prayer. She knew, not from the words of the shallow priest, but from the song that welled up in her soul. Her blessedness showed in her face: "Her countenance was no more sad" (1:18). Like Moses when he came down from the mount, she was not aware that her face shone (see Exodus 34:29). All she knew was that the hallelujahs of Heaven were the hymns of her heart. The glory of the Lord her God was upon her, as it had once been upon Jochebed.

Eli's caustic comment might well have turned to acid in Hannah's soul, soured her for the rest of her life, and turned her into another Peninnah. But nothing outward could affect her now. Her face told its own story of the peace of God reigning in her heart.

Hannah's blessedness also showed in her fruitfulness. Samuel was born! As she held that little bundle of humanity in her arms, she was thrilled through and through with gratitude to God.

The Spirit of God, who delights to dwell on details, tells how the child was named. Hannah "called his name Samuel, saying, Because I have asked him of the Lord" (1 Samuel 1:20). It would be so easy for her to forget that she had promised to give her baby to God, but she chose the name *Samuel* ("Asked of God") on purpose no doubt so that every time she called his name, she would be reminded of her promise.

The Holy Spirit also tells us how the child was nourished. "I will not go up until the child be weaned," Hannah said when her husband asked her if she was going to the annual feast (1:22). There is a lesson in Hannah's response. Sometimes it is far more important for a mother to stay at home than to attend a church service. Of course we must not underestimate the importance of church gatherings because God has commanded us to be present (Exodus 23:17; Hebrews 10:25). Indeed the Lord has promised to be present Himself on such occasions (Matthew 18:20). Even so, it is at times better for a mother to stay at home to ground her small children in the things of God than to hire baby sitters and run here and there to church functions.

With Hannah, staying at home was not an excuse, it was a spiritual exercise undertaken before God. She loved the gatherings of the Lord's people. For her not to go was an act of self-denying love, which is quite a different thing from negligence.

Hannah's blessedness showed in her face, in her fruitfulness, and in her faithfulness. She did all she could to guide her little lad's early steps aright. Then the time came when she had to fulfill her promise to God. But how could she tangibly give Samuel to Him? There was only one way she could think of: take him to the tabernacle and leave him with the high priest.

We can almost hear Satan whispering to Hannah: "What a foolish thing to do! Remember how harshly Eli spoke to you. Look at the mess he has made of raising his own sons. Think of what he'll do with yours. You can do better yourself. Keep him at home."

But Hannah and Elkanah "slew a bullock" (1 Samuel 1:25). In so doing they put their child under the blood and claimed the coming victory of Calvary. Then they "brought the child to Eli." Hannah said to him, "For this child I prayed" (1:27). And we can be sure that she continued to pray daily and hourly for Samuel.

God's solution to Israel's apostasy was a baby boy. When God could not find a man, He raised up a godly, praying woman who was willing to be the handmaiden of the Lord—willing to bring His solution into the world, and willing to consecrate herself to the spiritual training of the child. Her job was time-consuming, but greatly rewarding!

Years ago I met a man in Denver who was a missionary in Salt Lake City. He told me that every Monday morning two hundred young people leave from the Mormon temple to begin a two-year tour of duty on the missionfield. Before any young Mormon can go into business, he has to serve as a missionary for two years. As soon as a child is born, a Mormon father has to start setting aside money (in addition to his tithe) to support that child during his stint on the missionfield. Is it any wonder that the Mormons are erecting "350 church-size meetinghouses a year"?[3]

When we become as desperate as Hannah and as serious as the Mormons about winning souls, God will send us a Samuel or a John Wesley and revival.

---

1. Herbert Asbury, *A Methodist Saint: The Life of Bishop Asbury* (New York: Knopf, 1927) 29.

2. Ibid.

3. *Time,* August 4, 1997, 54.

# 12
# David
# and His Giant

*1 Samuel 16:11,18; 17:20,28,34,40*

```
        I.   DAVID'S CALL
        II.  DAVID'S COMING
        III. DAVID'S COMPASSION
        IV.  DAVID'S CONFESSION
        V.   DAVID'S CONQUEST
```

With the exception of the Lord Jesus, more Scripture is devoted to David than to any other individual. He is mentioned in 1 Samuel, 2 Samuel, 1 Kings, 1 Chronicles, and seventy-five Psalms. He is the first person named in the New Testament after Christ, and he is the last person named in the New Testament except for Christ. Next to Joseph, David is the most Christlike man in the Bible. Nowhere does this fact shine more brightly than in the section of 1 Samuel that tells about David and Goliath.

When we think of David, we think of a shepherd. As a youth he tended sheep and until the end of his days he had a shepherd's (pastor's) heart. For that reason he is set forth in the Old Testament as the ideal king. God's intention was that the prince should be the pastor of his people.

Five major types of shepherds are mentioned in the Old Testament. The first type is represented by Abel, the *righteous shepherd*.

The first two men born on this planet were both religiously inclined, but there was all the difference in the world in their understanding of what was needed in order to approach God. Cain, whose ideas could be summed up in the word "self," believed that his own good works were enough to please God and merit salvation. The first liberal thinker in the history of God's people, he set aside God's revealed word and put his own religious thinking in its place. Like all the world's false religions ever since, Cain's religion propagated the doctrine that salvation can be earned, that it can be purchased with blood, sweat, and tears. So he brought God the work of his hands and the fruit of a sin-cursed earth. No doubt his flower-draped, fruit-laden altar looked beautiful, but God rejected it.

Abel, whose beliefs could be summed up in the word "sacrifice," understood that he did not merit salvation. From the flock he lovingly tended, he brought a young lamb to the altar and shed its blood as an atonement for his sin.

God recorded that Abel was righteous. Cain was only religious. The two brothers were as different as Heaven and Hell.

The second type of shepherd is represented by Jacob, the *resourceful shepherd,* who had keen insight into the laws of genetics. His father and grandfather had been shepherds before him, but the shepherd instinct seems to have been stronger in Jacob than in Abraham and Isaac. In Jacob's hands, a lamb could gain a hundred pounds in a hundred days. Jacob knew how to mind sheep, mature sheep, and multiply sheep and those skills endeared him to his Uncle Laban.

The third type of shepherd is represented by Joseph, the *rejected shepherd.* As his father's well-beloved son, he occupied a unique position in the family. He was set apart from his brothers by birth, behavior, and benediction. He communed with his earthly father and always pleased his heavenly Father. But Joseph learned his shepherding in a hard school. He had to endure the wickedness and taunts of his half brothers, who hated him because of his character, conduct, convictions, and conversation. Like Jesus, "he came unto his own, and his own received him not" (John 1:11). Hoping never to see him again, they sold him for the price of a slave and callously handed him over to the Gentiles.

The fourth type of shepherd is represented by Moses, the *returning shepherd.* Having been rejected by the children of Israel, he became a shepherd in the desert. He assumed the shepherd character and in that character was given a Gentile bride. Raising a family apart from his kinsmen, Moses was a perfect type of Christ.

In the meantime the Hebrew people suffered great tribulation in Egypt as the threat of extermination continued to hang over their heads. They groaned in horror because of the great darkness and desolation that had overtaken them. They had rejected Moses, remained strangers to him, and spoken contemptuously about him. But back he came with the rod of power in his hand to pour out judgment miracles on Egypt and smite its sovereign, and to lead Israel to the promised land.

The fifth type of shepherd is represented by David, the *royal shepherd.* "A man after God's own heart," the shepherd-king was the gold standard by which all the other kings of the tribe of Judah were measured. They were deemed good or bad according to the degree that they were like David, who had a true heart for the flock.

The kings of the northern kingdom, on the other hand, were compared to the wretched standard set by "Jeroboam the son of Nebat, who made Israel to sin." All the northern kings followed in his wayward steps.

King Saul, David's predecessor in the united kingdom, did not have a shepherd's heart. When we first meet him, he is in charge of some donkeys and even them he manages to lose! (See 1 Samuel 9:3.)

# I. DAVID'S CALL

David's basic call was that of a shepherd. Five times in the story of David and Goliath (recorded in 1 Samuel 17) David is referred to as a shepherd. When Israel was forced to face the supreme test of the giant of Gath, they were as sheep without a shepherd. Then David came!

First Samuel 16 tells what happened before Goliath appeared on the scene. Samuel went down to the farm at Bethlehem to choose a king from among Jesse's sons, and the older boys were paraded one by one before the old prophet. Never before had he seen such good looking, healthy young men. He took one look at Eliab, the oldest and most impressive of them all, and said, "Surely the Lord's anointed is before him" (16:6).

God immediately answered, "Look not on his countenance, or on the height of his stature; because I have refused him: for the Lord seeth not as man seeth; for man looketh on the outward appearance, but the Lord looketh on the heart" (16:7). It seems that Eliab was an exact replica of Saul, whom Israel had chosen to be king because he was tall. But God is never impressed by a man's size. Eliab was no more useful than Saul was in the valley of Elah when Goliath challenged Israel.

One after another, Jesse's older sons were presented to Samuel, and God rejected all seven of them. The prophet was puzzled. "Are here all thy children?" he asked (16:11).

Jesse's answer was significant: "There remaineth yet the youngest, and, behold, he keepeth the sheep."

Samuel said to Jesse, "Send and fetch him: for we will not sit down till he come hither." All David's older brothers and even his father were made to stand, as if waiting for a king, until David came. Then Samuel set him in the midst of them and anointed him to be the next king of Israel.

Thus David was called to be the shepherd of the people of God. The sympathy, skill, and strength of character that David had developed while looking after the sheep on the hills were the same sympathy, skill, and strength of character that he would need to pastor the children of Israel. No man is fit to rule others until he has learned to be a shepherd of the sheep.

## II. DAVID'S COMING

The next scene in our study is set in the valley of Elah. The Philistines had a new champion, Goliath of Gath, who was a giant. God's people trembled before the might of this formidable foe. They had been troubled by the Philistines for a long time and had lost ground to them more often than not. Now the Israelites were paralyzed by fear.

The Philistines, being uncircumcised, had no part or lot with God's covenantal people. But there they were, in a place that belonged exclusively to God's redeemed people. In the typology of the Old Testament, the Philistines represent unsaved individuals who mingle among God's people and who have no right to occupy positions of power and authority in the church. They have come in by the back door, not by God's way. They may be leaders in the church, but they are really avowed enemies of God.

The Philistines were unsaved. On the other hand, God had put His people under the blood, brought them through the water, and baptized them unto Moses in the cloud. God had fed His people with manna from Heaven, given them water from the rock, and taught them how to have victory over Amalek (the flesh). God had directed His people to Sinai and, making His high and holy standards known to them, had shown them how a redeemed people should live. He had gathered them around the table in the tabernacle and led them step by step through the wilderness. Bringing them across the Jordan river, He had demonstrated the positional truths of death, burial, and resurrection. Then at Gilgal, God had instructed them to bring the cutting edge of Calvary to bear on the flesh.

The Philistines were in the promised land too, but they had arrived some other way. The place belonged to God's blood-bought people, but the Philistines used all the worldly means at their disposal to establish themselves in positions of power. They had taken the sword (a type of God's Word) away from Israel. Even if a man just wanted a hoe sharpened, he had to go to a Philistine to get it done. Goliath, now holding the sword in his hand, claimed to have the authority represented by the sword, just as modern liberals claim to be authorities on God's Word.

For years God's people had bowed before the clever, resourceful, and mighty Philistines. There had been spasmodic times of revival, and there had been a glimmering of hope under Samson, but he turned out to be too much of a playboy and overgrown schoolboy to bring any lasting deliverance from the foe. Samson was able to annoy the Philistines, but they soon discovered his weakness and used a woman to bait him so that they could blind and bind him. There had been even more hope under Samuel, but he soon became too busy—running here, there, and everywhere—to be able to deal permanently with the Philistine menace.

Now the Philistines were openly seeking a decisive, once-for-all victory over God's people. These enemies of Israel had on their side a giant, a veritable antichrist who was stamped all over with the number six. One of the sons of the Anakim, he was the devil's man arrayed in gleaming iron. Needless to say, Saul was no match for him. Neither was anyone else. David's older brother Eliab wasn't. Jonathan wasn't.

There was a climate of failure in Israel. The priesthood had failed under Eli, the prophets had failed under Samuel, and the monarchy had failed under Saul. Saul had faced the Philistines (the world), Amalek (the flesh), and Goliath (the devil)—and had failed each test.

Then God sent David, just as the Father would one day send Jesus. David came with the oil of the Holy Spirit upon him; he was the anointed one, just as Jesus would be. Jesse's son was a type and forerunner of Christ. (The name *Jesse* means "God is.")

"And David rose up early in the morning, and left the sheep with a keeper, and took, and went, as Jesse had commanded him: and he came to the trench, as the host was going forth to the fight, and shouted for the battle" (1 Samuel 17:20). All the Israelite army did was shout. Shouting did not defeat the Philistines then, and no victory is gained today when people merely make noise against liberalism in the church.

David did not shout. He came as a shepherd. The lion of the tribe of Judah was not yet to be revealed. It was as a shepherd that David met and mastered Goliath.

Let us never forget that God's answer to all that today's "Philistines" stand for is the Shepherd. His undershepherds must enter the battle too. The fight against liberalism is entrusted to those who have the pastor's heart and simply will not allow the flock to be attacked by people like Goliath and his crowd.

Jesus also came as a shepherd. He did not come the first time with fanfare and flourish, "with a shout, with the voice of the archangel, and with the trump of God" (1 Thessalonians 4:16). He did not come as a lion to roar and rend. He came as the Good Shepherd to give His life for the sheep.

## III. DAVID'S COMPASSION

As David greeted his brothers, he heard Goliath's roar and marveled that no one was doing anything to put an end to the outrageous situation. "Who is this uncircumcised Philistine, that he should defy the armies of the living God?" David demanded (1 Samuel 17:26).

Within the hour, David had to face the scoffing of three critics: Eliab, Saul, and Goliath. Eliab was the home critic; he questioned David's motives. Saul was the official critic; he questioned David's means. Goliath was the enemy critic; he questioned David's might. David had one answer to all three: God!

First David had to face Eliab, who had the true envious-elder-brother spirit. "Why camest thou down hither?" he asked. "With whom hast thou left those few sheep in the wilderness? I know thy pride, and the naughtiness of thine heart" (17:28). Eliab was filled with resentment that David, not he, was the Lord's anointed. Familiarity had bred contempt and out of the abundance of his unbelieving heart, Eliab had spoken.

The Lord Jesus, that great Shepherd of the sheep, also had to face his home critics. Not one of His brothers believed on Him until after He died and rose from the dead.

David's answer to his older brother was full of quiet dignity. Learning to hold his tongue was not the least of David's victories. James 3:2 says that if a man can bridle his tongue, he is perfect and can rule his whole body. So when Eliab asked what he was doing at the battlefront, David simply replied, "Is there not a cause?" (1 Samuel 17:29) In other words, "Nothing happens by chance." We could amplify David's answer as follows:

> It is not by chance I was born into Jesse's family, the family of a man whose name affirms "God is." It is not by chance that I have seven older brothers. It is not by chance that I have had to fight for my place in the family—not with carnal weapons but with spiritual ones. It is not by chance that I learned early to love, trust, and obey the living God. It is not by chance that God has become my constant companion and guide. It is not by chance that I learned to play the harp and write great hymns of the faith. Such things do not happen by chance; they happen by choice. God chose me, and I chose Him.
>
> It is not by chance that I became a shepherd and developed a heart for the flock. It is not by chance that

God gave me courage to face the lion and the bear in the wilderness of which you speak. It is not by chance that I have great skill with a sling and a stone. That skill represents hard work and constant practice. And it is not by chance that I'm not afraid of Goliath and you are.

Likewise it is not by chance that we are where we are and that we are who we are.

David probably left much unsaid because his compassion was that of a shepherd. He loved Eliab and wanted to save him along with everyone else.

## IV. DAVID'S CONFESSION

In due time David was brought before King Saul. Saul looked him up and down and said, "Thou art not able to go against this Philistine to fight with him: for thou art but a youth, and he a man of war from his youth" (1 Samuel 17:33).

Remember, King Saul knew David. David was his chief musician. He had been hired to play the harp to soothe Saul's soul when it was tormented by an unclean spirit. David's credentials had been checked at the time. In fact he had been highly recommended by one of Saul's servants, who had said, "I have seen a son of Jesse the Beth-lehemite, that is cunning in playing [his competence], and a mighty valiant man [his courage], and a man of war [his conquests], and prudent in matters [his caution], and a comely person [his charisma], and the Lord is with him [his character]" (16:18).

But Saul seems to have forgotten David's good credentials. All he saw was a teenager with a handsome face, an earnest manner, and an eager spirit. Saul had also seen Goliath and as usual had judged by outward appearances. "Thou art but a youth, and he a man of war from his youth," Saul said. So David confessed to victories he had previously kept secret:

Thy servant kept his father's sheep, and there came a lion, and a bear, and took a lamb out of the flock.... Thy servant slew both the lion and the bear: and this uncircumcised Philistine shall be as one of them, seeing he hath defied the armies of the living God (17:34-36).

However, David's trust was in God, not in his own prowess. David's trust reminds us of Jesus' reliance on His Father. As man, our Lord made Himself wholly available to His Father as God; His Father, as God, made Himself wholly available to Jesus as man. Jesus was never anything less than God over all, blessed for evermore. However, as man, Jesus was dependent on His Father. Moment by moment, situation by situation, Jesus yielded to His Father in Heaven. He expects us to do the same.

## V. DAVID'S CONQUEST

Impressed by David's utter fearlessness, Saul decided to let David go into the valley. But first Saul arrayed him in his armor. He must have been a sight to behold—a slim youth decked out in Saul's heavy panoply of brass and iron! David could barely stand up in it, let alone walk. Besides, he was not about to fight the enemy with Saul's worldly weapons. And like David's weapons, "the weapons of our warfare are not carnal, but mighty through God to the pulling down of strong holds" (2 Corinthians 10:4).

David took Saul's armor off. Then "he took his staff in his hand, and chose him five smooth stones out of the brook, and put them in a shepherd's bag" (1 Samuel 17:40). His conquest was to be that of a shepherd—the shepherd who had written the twenty-third Psalm. David's "sling was in his hand: and he drew near to the Philistine."

Goliath came cursing, boasting, and blaspheming the living God, and David answered with a confident statement that committed the whole contest to God (17:45-47). One can well believe that David's peerless words from Psalm 23:4 also echoed across that valley:

> Yea, though I walk through death's dark vale,
> Yet will I fear no ill;
> For Thou art with me, and Thy rod
> And staff me comfort still.[1]

Back went David's hand and straight to its mark flew the stone. Suddenly it was all over! Five thousand shekels of brass rang out Goliath's death knell as he fell headlong to the ground. David was upon him in a flash. Using the giant's sword, he hewed off Goliath's head and thus destroyed "him that had the power of death" (see Hebrews 2:14).

There stood David with Goliath's mighty sword in one hand and his gory head in the other. Never again would that giant wield his sword against God's sword. Never again would he blaspheme the living God. From that fight David returned victorious and all God's people sang and shouted his fame.

Tradition holds that David took Goliath's head to Jerusalem, that it was buried in a place known as *Gal Goliah,* and that the site became known in Jesus' day as *Golgotha,* "the place of the skull." If that is so, someone mightier than David won an even mightier victory over an even more dreadful foe at the place where the head of the Philistine is buried. In any case, Christ is the ultimate answer to all the teachings of the "Goliaths" who have infiltrated the church.

---

1. From the *Scottish Psalter.*